Shades of Colour

The Tribal in Indian Fiction

Harsh Vardhan Khimta

WKRISHIND

Nature's Creation

Shades of Colour

Harsh Vardhan Khimta

Wkrishind Publishers
WKRISHIND.IN

Publication Date: December 2023
Edition: I

Harsh Vardhan Khimta
Shimla, Himachal Pradesh
WKRISHIND.IN

To The Subordinated.

Contents

Chapter - 1

Various Aspects of the Subaltern Question

History of this great nation of ours from Jambudvupa to Bharat to India has been a timeless one through history, geography and civilisation. Ironically or otherwise, the people & their cultures have also been looked up in these different zones of time & political entity. A look at the following article written in the winter of 1901, at the peak of the British Empire makes it clear. A foreign correspondent reporting from the summer capital of the empire at Simla for The New York Times wrote an article which was unambiguously titled *Wild Tribes of India Becoming Civilized: Lord Curzon's Trip Through Remote Districts.* The trip in question was undertaken through the 'wilds of Assam, Manipur and Upper Assam." The report reads, "It is the first time that any ruler of India has gone so far from the beaten track. Ten years ago such a journey would have been impossible. The hill tribes were then untamed, treacherous savages. Manipur had but recently risen and slaughtered the British resident and the chief commissioner of Assam.... The people throughout, including the half wild Chins from the almost unknown regions bordering on China, have received Lord Curzon with loyalty and marked enthusiasm, and have not been slow to testify to the peaceful benefits of British rule in a country where but a few years since every man's hand was raised against his neighbour." This article appearing in The New York Times on December 22 1901 was a vindication of the empire that had done so much as to civilise the savage tribes within ten years.

Such descriptions of the subjects of the empire were common in the days when it was natural to call the natives 'wild' and 'savage' without any reasonable consideration, leave alone sensitivity towards the repercussions such portrayal could have for them. Having begun with the assertion that the wild tribes were becoming civilised under the empire and had started reaping the 'peaceful benefits of the British rule' it goes on to describe what seems to be the real motive of the article It laments the fact that vast wealth of the hills, along the entire Himalayan range from Kumaon and Garhwal to Nepal and then to Assam, Manipur and Burma, has gone unexploited due to lack of means of communication and transportation. The natural wealth includes timber, petroleum, gold, minerals such as copper and lead, precious stones, sapphires, gold-bearing rivers and orchids which would be worth their weight in gold in London'.

Such writing by non-native & for an international readership is typical of the time when the empire, having civilised the wild treacherous tribes within ten years, should now have the legitimate right to the vast natural wealth of the region which would now be possible since the viceroy's trip would accelerate the effort to set railways and communication lines through the hills tracks, a task that would not be too difficult to carry out since the local labour is described as "docile and easy to be trained and food 'cheap and in abundance." That was the time when Kipling could write, without scruples, about a paharı girl Lisbeth, who, 'being a savage by birth took no trouble to hide her feelings' as she had the stupidity of falling in love with an Englishman who was made of 'superior clay' and who was later beaten by her native husband regularly after the manner of the Paharis (Kipling 9-14). It was such ambling through literary discourse, with serious repercussions on historiography, that begs the modern-day reader of a willing suspension of disbelief of a much inferior kind.

What is the subjectivity of the tribal population of India and what are the issues related to its representation in the various media, fiction in particular? Subjectivity refers to a subject's perspective, particular feelings, beliefs and desires. It is often used casually to refer to unjustified personal opinions, in contrast to knowledge and justified belief. In philosophy, the term is often contrasted with objectivity (Solomon 900) It is, therefore, the tribal identity culture, traditions, social and political standing, and above all the aspirations of the tribal society that form the core of tribal subjectivity. All these factors that determine the subjectivity of a people refer to their relative position in society and sometimes even determine that position. Continuing further with the description of subjectivity as given by Solomon, "In social science, subjectivity (the property of being a subject) is an effect of relation of power. Similar social configurations create similar perceptions, experiences and interpretations of the world. For example, female subjectivity would refer to the perceptions, experiences and interpretations that a generally have of the world" (900).

It is the 'individual' that forms the centre stage of the study since, "... it is a mistake for philosophy to relegate subjectivity to being merely a function of something else, such as language, ideology, history, or the unconscious" (Bowil 8); also "scientific method and bureaucratic rarionalization actually attempts to exclude the individual subject in the name of 'objectivity' whereas 'subjectivity is the attempt of the I to describe itself (Bowil 20). "Representation of a certain class, society or a people and the 'image' formed in the popular psyche as a result of such representation play a pivotal role in determining its place in relation to its surroundings. It is through the representation of a particular group of people or society through the various agencies of print and visual media that their perception in the minds of other people is formed. In literary theory representation is commonly defined in three ways: "... to look like or resemble, to stand in for something someone and to present a second time, to re-present" (O'Shaughnessy and Stadler 28).

It [representation] is, " an extremely elastic notion, which extends all the way from a stone representing a man to a novel representing the day in the life of several Dubliners" (Mitchell 67). The form of representation under consideration here is literary, that is, the description of certain groups of people or society in popular literature. Mitchell quotes Aristotle who describes representation in three ways; The Object. the symbol being represented, Manner the way the symbol is represented; and Means: the material that is used to represent it, and the means of literary representation is language (67) Literary creativity is an important form of representation since, 'representation' is the ability of texts to draw upon features of the world and present them to the viewer, not simply as reflection, but more so, as constructions" (Shaughnessy 28). The group in question here is the tribal population of India and the genre of literary creation is fiction.

Such representation of the tribal people should be a worrying factor because they have, by and large, rarely been represented truthfully and, therefore, have hardly ever been understood sympathetically and completely as Arundhati Roy says, "...the politics of 'representation is complicated and fraught with danger and dishonesty" (16). Most of the tribal societies in India possessed no script and ne writing or documenting activity as such. Most of their experiences, "histories" and cultural aspects find expression in their folklore and other oral traditions. It was thus inevitable that these societies were mostly 'represented in the writings of the outsiders, be they the traders, missionaries, government officials or travelers. And since no such source could have been entirely devoid of bias, the tribal society came to be known through various such narratives most of which were coloured by the presenter's own notions and prejudice.

The tribal society has mostly been on the receiving end of such mindless portrayals. Talking for instance of the views held by the mainstream society of the nature of tribal uprisings throughout the colonial period, Ranajit Guha condemned:

...careless and impressionistic writing on the subject of [tribal and peasant] insurrections being purely spontaneous and unpremeditated affairs. The truth is quite to the contrary It would be difficult to cite an uprising on any significant scale that was not in fact preceded either by less militant types of mobilization when other means had been tried and found wanting or by parley among its principals seriously to weigh the pros and cons of any recourse to arms (Guha 1).

Such writings, argues Guha, at best carried out the task of 'giving lie to the myth' (1).

Guha quotes numerous examples of tribal and peasant mutinies against the colonial oppressors after their methods of peaceful negotiations had failed. He thus contradicts the claim of colonial administrative writings and records that suggest such impulsive retaliation and [Guha] maintains that " "...there is hardly any instance of ...the volatile adivasis stumbling or drifting into rebellion since they had too much on stake and would not launch into it except as a deliberate, even if desperate, way out of an intolerable condition of existence" (1).

It is the negation of this 'consciousness' that has been ignored in the annals of times and the tribal is shown to us as someone who is often rebellious in nature without much reason for the same as Ranajit Guha quotes the first historian of the Chuar Rebellion of 1779, J.C. Price who talks of, 'those periodical outbursts of crime and lawlessness to which all wild tribes are subject (3). Such historians and other writers played an important role in convincing the colonial administration of the violent nature of the tribes and provided them the pretext 'to intervene, to evangelize and civilize natives' (Kalpana Ram 78). The enactment of The Criminal Tribes Act of 1871 was a barbaric culmination of such misrepresentation, dovetailed with the insatiable greed of the empire for natural resources and abundant bonded labour. Ranajit Guha notes with dismay:

Yet this consciousness seems to have received little notice in the literature on the subject. Historiography has been content to deal with the peasant rebel merely as an empirical person or member of a class, but not as an entity whose will and reason constituted the praxis called rebellion. The omission is indeed dyed into most narratives by metaphors assimilating peasant revolts to natural phenomena they break out like thunder storms, heave like earthquakes, spread like wildfires, infect like epidemics. [suggesting] a very low state of civilization....How did historiography come to acquire this particular blind spot and never find a cure (2)?

Guha examines in detail two texts, examples of primary sources, which reflect upon the colonial interpretation of tribal insurgencies, related to the Barasat uprising of 1831 and Santal rebellion of 1855. Imperial government's official correspondence refers to peasants as "insurgents committing the most daring and wanton atrocities on the inhabitants of the country" (4). He demonstrates how the colonial state interpreted intention to punish oppressors as 'intention to attack', and struggle for a better social order as 'disturbing the public tranquillity' About the Santal rebellion, which was an uprising to establish self rule and dignity, the government is dismissive as:

...it is their intention to attack all the Europeans round and plunder and murder them. The cause of all this is that one of their Gods is supposed to have taken the Flesh and to have made his appearance at some place near this, and that it is his intention to reign as a King overall this part of India, and had ordered the Sontals to collect and put to death all the Europeans and influential Natives around (6)

Re-reading such representations against the background of colonialism one can "...detect chinks which have allowed 'comment', to worm its way through the plate armour of fact and such primary reports [are] the voice of committed colonialism" (13). The modern historian, investigating the reports of the colonial establishment has to read them against the grain as Shahid Amin warns, "It is, quite important for any historian of the subaltern classes to investigate the discursive practices within which statements by the police, administrators, judges, and by the accused themselves, are produced most statements about the dominated are produced within weil-defined fields of power" (167).

It is within the high and such clearly impenetrable walls of power that the subaltern and those on the wrong side of power are represented and their very cause is questioned. It is through such imposed representation that they are made to seem to be pursuing a wrong course of action and thus their defeat and destruction is easy to cause and justify.

Guha observes, "What comes out of the interplay of these mutually implied but opposed matrices is that our texts are not the record of observations uncontaminated by bias, judgment and opinion. On the contrary, they speak of a total complicity (15) Upon closer examination of the official records of the period, it becomes abundantly clear how most of such movements or agitations by the local inhabitants, tribals being still more vulnerable, were treated as unruly behavior, to unreasonably cause disturbance to the larger sections of the public. Once classified as villainous, they had no scruples in putting them down mercilessly.

In his introductory address to participants of the national seminar on The Tribal Situation in India held at the Indian Instute of Advanced Study at Shimla in 1972, Niharranjan Ray gave a detailed analysis of the word 'tribe' without failing to enquire whether such definition met the relevant social situation in India. Throwing light on the word 'tribe' he said:

Derived from a Latin root, the Middle English term tribuz meaning the three divisions into wluch the early Romans were grouped, came to evolve into the modern English 'tribe' With the Romans, the 'tribe' was a political division while the Greeks seem to have equated it somewhat with their 'fraternities' at times, with geographical division at others. In Irish history however, the term meant families or communities of persons having the same surname. In certain other areas of the western world and certain periods of history, it stood for a division of terrritory allotted to a family or community Today with anthropologists and sociologists of western origin the term means, according to latest edition of the Oxford Dictionary, "a race of people; now applied especially to a primary aggregate of people in a primitive or barbarous condition, under a headman or chief." It is in this meaning, roughly speaking, that most of the western scholars working on India, have been using this term, with but slight change of emphasis here and there (8)

Definition of tribe and, therefore, what constitutes 'tribalism', have not always been such a matter of fact From Sarat Chandra Roy for whom aboriginal tribe ... was essentially pure, simple and isolated whose culture was rude and primitive' (Dasgupta 148) to Spivak's rejection of these terms as 'neither aboriginal nor tribal fits the Indian case' (327), who [Spivak] prefers to use Scheduled Tribes as laid down in the Indian Constitution, and regularly used by the state and activists alike' (327), the tribal terminology has travelled a long way. Between being identified as criminals by birth by the British in 1871 and therefore 'dishonoured by history' (Radhakrishna 2001) to being denotified by the Republic of India, the adivasi population of India has been at times condemned as savage, condescended upon as backward or patronised as natural.

It could conveniently he said that in the beginning, the entire world should necessarily have been 'tribal'. By tribal is meant an environment that had smaller groups of people, united by a common lineage and background, living together and often in conflict with other groups over territory, and resources such as food, water and shelter. Also, the term means subsistence level of existence when just the bare necessities were thought to be necessary to be satisfied. Also, it meant little or no control over the raw forces of nature as far as self-protection from such forces was concerned.

The earlier histories of nations and histories of geography tell us, as described in detail by Nayan Chanda in his book Bound Together How Traders, Preachers, Adventurers, and Warriors Shaped Globalization (2007) of various nomadic tribes of certain regions travelling over to another region and in the process encountering resistance (both natural and human), losing and gaining characteristics, shedding and imbibing different values, conquering and being defeated, multiplying and mixing, accepting and sharing, some settling down and some moving still on. Some of these settlements grew larger with time and in the process developed such norms of life that differentiated them from their way of earlier living. Philosophy, art, music, and more sophisticated methods of cultivation were born and developed.

There still remained two things, with development of which a society made the steadiest 'progress' from their earlier forms to the newer ones. First was the organisation on larger scales. This is when more groups knitted themselves into still larger groups, overlooking (to an increasingly larger extent) lineage, background and geography. This organisation led to the formation and strengthening of smaller settlements into larger societies, societies into towns, states and nations. This enriched these organised entities (who in the process evolved for themselves common philosophies, norms and common ambitions) with a formidable unified force. This force soon turned into sophisticated power, with which, if nothing else, ambitions had to be fulfilled.

Secondly, along with the process of organising came the need and the urge to develop means to overcome the common obstacles to everyday existence that were thrown up by the forces of nature. This effort to overcome natural obstacles was essentially to safeguard oneself from starvation to begin with, and then to develop means of protection from rain, cold, heat, floods, darkness, beasts, enemies, diseases and accidents.

These societies, writes Benoy Kumar Sarkar, drawing form Gumplowicz:

> *...were held together by material interests. In due course different groups coalesce to form states. The impetus for state formation originates in the desire to subjugate others, which in turn leads to assimilation with the subjugated groups, and finally to amalgamation with them. This, according to*

Gumplowicz, is the process by which nations or 'folk states' are formed (Chatterjee 118).

Throughout human history this mutual existence did not always go on peacefully as different groups or states continued to be in a state of competition with the other, as:

World history ... can be thought of in terms of an interaction between vishwa-shakti or world forces' and human will. The important points that Sarkar took from the two western thinkers, Gumplowicz and Ratzenhofer, are that material interest provides the dynamic force behind social evolution, such interests lead to conflict between social evolution, that conflict is a creative force in history and that there is no such thing as infinite progress- all societies go through cycles of progression and regression (119).

With the passage of time great nation states were carved out of huge geographical areas. Along with it religions and thus civilisations spread across many areas and peoples. During this long evolving process certain groups remained isolated and continued to exist and flourish in their own vicinities, mostly in the forests, hills or islands. They retained their characteristics of the earlier times, much to the surprise of the modern day anthropologists, as acknowledged by Sarat Chandra Roy in his 1937 paper The study of anthropology from the Indian view-point that the, '....primitive society exhibits the ground-plan on which the more complex structure that we call civilization has been built up'(Dasgupta 138). This view point was later echoed by Benoy Kumar Sarkar in The Political Philosophies Since 1905 in 1942 Sarkar talks of Bengali culture as the product of a continuous process of acculturation, first with the conquering Vedic Indo-Aryans, and later with the Buddhists and Hindus from Bihar, Punjab, and Kanauj. He says that Bengali culture was invented by pariahs: "the aboriginals living in hills, forests and river valleys, as well as the untouchable and depressed classes and some of the lower castes, nay, many of those castes who have in subsequent ages got admitted into the alleged higher castes..." (Chatterjee 119-120). In due course of time, the larger and comparatively better organized societies came to view their lesser cultured and not as effectively organised counterparts as less advantaged and the term tribe that may once have covered almost all of humanity was now restricted to them alone. The term tribal assumed different connotations and its implications and significance too continued to undergo changes.

Then should have followed the search to reduce 'inconvenience' met with in day-today life, new methods may have been devised to avoid unpleasant experiences of life and efforts to make life more livable. Finally may have arisen the need for leisure and thirst for more pleasure, which are also attainable at the most subsistence level of existence, such as drinking, dancing, singing, sex, smoking etc. The search for leisure and the quest for pleasure at this level inevitably involve winning control over nature and by developing newer methods of subjugating her forces to human experience. This powerful human experience is what we can call knowledge.

It is knowledge and power, the combination of which, especially when applied to fuel desire and ambition has made all the difference, It is this that differentiates one set of people from other As Michel Foucault's Discipline and Punish The Birth of the Prison (1977), has argued convincingly, knowledge and power compliment each other. One leads to another and also, one is the result of the other. Foucault's understanding of the issue is summed up in his own words:

Power produces knowledge, Power and knowledge directly imply one another. There is no power relation without the correlative constitution of a field of knowledge, nor any knowledge that does not presuppose and constitute at the same time power relations. These 'power-knowledge relations are to be analyzed on the basis of the subjects who know, the objects to be known, and the modalities of knowledge must be regarded as so many effects of these fundamental implications of power-knowledge and their historical transformations (28).

The so-called tribal or the aboriginal population today comprises, by and large, of those who have been left behind in the race of development. The word tribe associated with them is used at times to refer to the historical traits that are understood to have had an important impact not just on their society but also on those who came in touch with them through interaction or confrontation. Despite the best intentions of many such authors and commentators, the terminology has often been used in an irresponsible manner which further discourages the cause of these already disadvantaged societies since proliferation of such information only defeats their cause in the consciousness of the so-called mainstream society.

The comparatively smaller tribal society had power and knowledge but in accordance with their way of living and it was limited to the level of subsistence. They lacked the third important ingredient of the subjugating societies, ie, magnitude. It was with relatively greater magnitude of power and knowledge that dominant national societies and cultures pushed others into relative slavery or oblivion. Most tribes in India, for all their civilisational and cultural richness, are thought to have been driven into the hills by the militarily powerful and organized Aryans. In the Indian context the term 'tribe' was introduced by the British administrators. In the words of Niharranjan Ray.

> *...they knew too well that India had been aspiring for nationhood, and the whole burden of their argument seems to have been that the people of India could not weld themselves into a nation so long as these two major hurdles (scheduled tribes and castes] were not removed. How true they were! But it was not to their interest to remove them, by their policy they only accentuated them and encouraged the divisive forces. Some of the so-called 'tribes' they chose, for administrative reasons and in the name of law and order", to brand as*

'criminal tribes, and as late as 1935, created the remarkable phrase and social category called 'scheduled tribes' along with another called 'scheduled castes', two phrases and concepts that we inherited from the 1935 Constitution of the independent and sovereign Republic of India! (Ray 19-20).

The words 'tribal' and 'tribalism' have come to be associated with many traits, most of which are derogatory. The terms are mostly used carelessly and, therefore, do no justice to those who may be offended indirectly. Of course it was not the case with professional sociologists and anthropologists. Describing the Oraons of Chhota Nagpur, Sarat Chandra Roy equates the word 'tribalism with the 'tribal identity" Sangeeta Dasgupta lays out Roy's notion, " even as Roy viewed the tribe as somehow out of tune with time, conforming to the universal parameters of 'primitive society', he believed the Oraons were a historically constituted and therefore changing community. A disjuncture had appeared, and to explain it new designations and characterizations were employed. Thus Roy used, in addition to the category 'tribes', the term 'agricultural community' to describe the Oraons" (150).

Roy had, like few others, provided a legitimate check point to the dangers of careless or manipulative connotations the term would be vulnerable to in the future, Dasgupta quotes from Roy's article Types of Cultural Theory published in Man in India in 1921," the rigid determinism and a too absolute classification of the earlier evolutionist school which takes little account of tribal migrations and the transmission of cultural elements from one people or area to another and the intermixture of races and cultures, was soon found to be incompatible with all the ascertained ethnological facts... no hard and fast line could be always drawn between savagery, and barbarism and civilisation and the course of cultural advance has seldom proceeded in a straight line from one dominant sociological type to another....the evolutionary or psychological interpretation of cultural phenomenon as conditioned solely and absolutely by the psychological unity of mankind came to be regarded by many anthropologists as inadequate" (151).

Quoted here is a paragraph from Edward W. Said's Culture and Imperialism:

> *One should not pretend that modes for a harmonious world order are ready at hand, and it would be equally disingenuous to suppose that ideas of peace of community have much of a chance when power is moved to action by aggressive perception of vital national interests or unlimited sovereignty. We are all taught to venerate our nations and admire our traditions, we are taught to pursue their interests with toughness and in disagreed for other societies. 4 new and in my opinion appalling tribalism is fracturing societies, separating peoples, promoting greed, blooding confliet and uninteresting assertions of minor ethnic or group particularity Little time is spent not so much in 'learning about the cultures the phrase has*

an inane vagueness to it but in studying the map of interaction the actual and often productive traffic occurring on a day-by-day and even minute by-minute, basis among states, societies groups identities (italics mine) (20).

This appalling tribalism, according to Said is fracturing societies and separating people and what is more, tribalism is promoting greed and tribalism is promoting bloody conflict!

This is where the problem begins. Or, this is net result of a set of probiematic tendencies and attitudes and prejudices that colour the way the mainstream world looks and constructs the "Other" and in this case it happens to be the tribal. This depiction by the one such as Said (who happens to belong to the non-tribal society and is writing for the informed readers) is in many ways similar to the colonizer's attitude that inspires the basic arguments of the subalterns' interrogation. Despite Said's best intentions and somewhat innocence, a considerable amount of injustice still appears to have been done to those for whom 'tribalism' is not just a matter of identity but, more importantly, the very notion of being.

Pondering over Said's argument one wonders how 'tribalism' is necessarily fracturing societies and separating people? Or does tribalism symbolise a tendency that divides society? A review of the history of the world of the last two thousand years is enough to reiterate that the deepest and longest lasting chasms in the human race have been caused by religions, philosophies, cultural identities, notions of nationalism and self-interest of societies and nations. All these are understood to be non-tribal characteristics and symbolise an evolved mind. These tendencies no doubt have united large groups but at the same time have alienated and separated them from other large groups which have also been united by similar but contrary seeming tendencies. The greatest example is that religions, which are meant to help and reflect upon the essential unity of humankind, have resulted, though unintentionally, in some of the greatest divisions in our race. Tribal groups are divided on the basis of common ancestors and territory. They probably do not have divisions of our magnitude and damaging proportions.

Said further argues that this appalling tribalism "is promoting greed." The point here is to what extent is it correct to associate tribalism with greed? This would suggest that tribal societies have greed as one of their main characteristics. On the contrary, a study of the tribal life will demonstrate that, by and large, the tribal society as a whole is content within its limited geographical regions. Individuals are also more or less content with their self-sustainable life style on natural resources and restricted to subsistence.

The mainstream society, on the contrary, has a long history of aggression and aggrandisement as a part of the foreign policy, slave trade, empire building as the case may be causing the subjugation of weaker races by highly organised powers. The magnitude of greed in the mainstream and the so called civilised world is a truly appaling and disturbing phenomenon in the present times that needs to be addressed.

Another point of contestation in Said's commentary is his reference to the appalling tribalism held responsible for promoting bloody conflict. Again this human tendency of causing bloody conflict is traced back to the tribal way of life. These are sweeping generalisations made by the mainstream society that simply dismisses any negativity remotely connected to them, anything and everything that marks the difference from their main life style is dismissed as sub-human, barbaric and uncivilised. The generalisation is easily encouraged when the subject in question is a set of people who dwell in the remote forests and co-exist in perfect harmony with nature without any sophistication thus posting a challenge to the civilised man's ideological beliefs.

The history of the civilised world is uniformly marked by bloody conflicts owing to its deep divisions, conflicting ambitions and excessive greed. The "Union of Power and Knowledge" has been the greatest exploiter of weaker and less advanced nation states in our own day, USSR's march into Afghanistan in the 1980s and the USA's adventures in the Gulf are enough to substantiate that the most developed nation states are guilty of genocide and are violators of human rights. Their records in these fields are humane only within their national boundaries. Outside the domain of their nation they are the greatest schemers of wars, exploitation, loot and abuse, in the name of vital national interests. The twentieth century probably saw the most widespread bloodshed and atrocities against humanity in all the recorded history. In all this the greatest participation belongs to those who claim the highest level of advancement and civilisation.

Edward Said further says, "There is no question, for example, that in the past decade the extraordinarily intense reversion to tribal and religious sentiments all over the world has accompanied and deepened many of the discrepancies among polities that have continued since if they were not actually created by the period of high European imperialism"(20).

Here the phrase 'reversion to tribal religious sentiments' indicates that associating with the tribal way of life is necessarily a step backward. Backward in time? If that alone is intended. It's acceptable, for we believe that the world began as a 'tribal' in the sense that has already been argued, ie., divided into little groups, less organised and barely subsistent. But if the intentions to suggest that it is a step backwards in terms of 'reversion to greed, bloody conflict and conflicting divisions', the tone is inevitably offensive and derogatory and lacks genuine understanding of the far away pristine world of the tribals, so different otherwise.

This leads us to the initial problem of defining and subsequently understanding the tribal and tribalism. What does tribalism mean? The terms tribal and tribalism should indeed be associated with 'tribal identity' and the very essence of belonging to the tribal world. It is more of an associational and cultural entity rather than the baseness of human nature. Therefore, if "tribalism" means promotion of greed, bloody conflict, fracturing societies and separating people the so called mainstream civilised world is invariably more tribal than the hitherto categorically classified tribal races dwelling in forests and semi-forest areas around the world whe are still considered to be less civilised. In this context the word 'tribalism' should no longer be associated with those tribes. In fact the entity of a tribe should not just signify those smaller groups, linked together by common ancestors and lineage but it should entail the entire humanity which are at different stages in terms of their organisation and power and also in terms of their advancement in knowledge. On the contrary, if by 'tribalism' we mean the way of life of the so called tribes that still live in pockets around the world, we should completely discard associating this world with fracturing societies, separating peoples and promotion of bloody conflict and greed. Having the two together, i.e. associating 'tribalism' with the way of life of the still existing so called 'tribes and at the same time with bloody conflict, greed etc. would be arrogance and voluntarily depriving of real understanding of the subject.

Edward Said's statement therefore, can be re-framed as, "A new [if it really is new] and in my opinion appalling madness is fracturing societies, separating peoples, promoting greed, bloody conflict and un interesting assertions of minor ethnic or group particularity" (Italics mine).

It is only madness and misunderstanding that fracture societies and separate people. It is again madness that promotes greed and bloody conflict. This is madness not in the clinical sense of the term but in the sense of moral depravity and it is madness in a sense that corrupts human behavior and instigates it to deviate so drastically from the course of Human Spirit that epitomises co-operation, love and respect to others' right to live amidst others. The Algerian soldiers who did not speak French were declared mad and sent to mental asylums by the French doctors (see Frantz Fanon's The Wretched of the Earth, 1961). The tribal predicament is in no way different.

In a series of lectures on India to the future ICS officers at Cambridge, Max Muller says, "What I should wish to impress on those who will soon find themselves the rulers of millions of human beings in India, is the duty to shake off national prejudices, which are apt to degenerate into a kind of madness" (55).

This is the meaning of madness intended here. It is the result of degeneration of the human mind and the cause of which is prejudice which is caused when one belongs to a nation, race, culture or class that one thinks is necessarily superior to the others.

It is imperative to note here that this degeneration and moral depravity is simply not tribalism, if by tribal one means the way of life of the presently living so called tribes. This madness resulting from moral depravity and degeneration of human thought is a common human element and it assumes enormous magnitude and proportion especially when designed on the level of nation states, religions, and large scale cultural identities. And this madness is made more effective, penetrating and damaging when backed with power and knowledge. The means are enslavement and exploitation, and the ends are the pleasures of wealth, more power and continuing hegemony.

This further makes it imperative to redefine the word tribal and hence tribalism. The question now is should the term 'tribe' be continued to be in use, particularly despite the changes of over the last one century? Is it possible to do away with these clichés as they now are loaded with derogatory overtones and are, in the socio-cultural context, redundant and impasse. The International Encyclopedia of the Social Sciences (1968) enlightens us on the issues, "In general usage, the word 'tribe' is taken to denote a primary aggregate of people living in a primitive or barbarous condition under a headman or a chief" (146).

Here, calling these so called 'close' societies barbarous is highly questionable. Fortunately, the Encyclopedia further specifies:

The unnecessary moralistic overtones that this usage implies can be avoided or minimized by the use of the expression 'tribal society' which is to be preferred to such synonyms as 'primitive society' or 'preliterate society. At the same time, the word 'tribe' need not be discarded. Indeed, it has become a technical term denoting a territorially defined political unit, a usage that recalls the original Latin use of the word for the political divisions or patrician orders of the Roman State (146).

Therein lies the answer. The word tribe (and hence tribal) should continue to be used and understood as a technical term denoting a 'territorially defined political unit This would mean that the tribes are seen as a people who belong to different social and cultural environment, in addition to the territorial dimensions. The term needs to be completely washed off its 'moralistic overtones' as they are assumed arbitrarily and are used as tools of exploitation and prejudice.

Civilisation and culture are among some of the subversive agencies employed by mainstream societies for the purposes of representing/ misrepresenting the tribal societies. It is an irony that the vast majority of mankind that has long lost their closed kinship and group identities and has assumed the more sophisticated ways of existence into miniscule units of family have acquired the authority to look at the comparatively less advanced people as sub-humans or less civilised and in some cases as uncivilised.

While mentioning the manner of Bedoweens, or pastoral Arabs, Edward Gibbon writes in the Decline and Fall of the Roman Empire:

The measure of population is regulated by the means of subsistence, and the inhabitants of this vast peninsula might be outnumbered by the subjects of a fertile and industrious province. Along the shores of the Persian gulf, of the ocean (the India Ocean), and even the red sea, the Ichthyophagi, or fish eaters, continued to wander in quest of their precarious food. In this primitive and object state, which still deserves the name of society, the human brute, without arts or laws, almost without sense or language, is poorly distinguished from the rest of the animal creation. Generations and ages might roll away in silent oblivion, and the helpless savage was restrained

from multiplying his race by the wants and pursuits
which confined his existence to the narrow margins
of the sea coast (70).

It can be said that the wanderers in that age may not
have had well organised social systems but then to term
them 'human brute' in general is objectionable. Also,
they may have been without a language, i.e., a well
developed grammar and vocabulary, but to deny them
'sense' would be too arrogant and almost naïve.

An interesting case is found in Encyclopedia
Asiatica (1858, 1976) Describing the people of the hills
in British India, it stated, "Hill tribes is general term by
which the British designate collectively the numerous
uncivilized tribes who inhabit the mountain ranges and
higher hills in British India and along it borders. Most
of them are wholly illiterate" (45).

Further explaining the characteristics of these
'uncivilized hill tribes', Edward Balfour, the editor,
probably unconsciously, stumbles upon some facts
which he innocently puts down as...character
phlegmatic, good-humored, cheerful and tractable...
Crime rare, and they are truthful' (53). This is
paradoxical that on the one hand they are described as
non- criminals and quite truthful, and on the other hand
uncivilised. Moving on to the inhabitants of the valleys
of Kangra and Sutlej it is stated that these people are
sturdy, honest, independent, amenable and gentle and
free of low cunning The question remains as to how on
earth these people with the aforesaid attributes can ever
be denigrated as 'uncivilised.

Thus it could be inferred that the mainstream society, in its arrogance, comfortably concludes that those who are unlike them in terms of culture and history and less powerful are necessarily inferior This arrogance, coupled with global ambitions heaped on them on the pretext of the mission to civilise the rest without giving themselves a chance to evaluate those who did not resemble their way of life, resulted in brute force that the inperial governments used in order to further their cause. This is true not just of the European colonising adventures or to say the least, the misadventures in the colonies over the last few centuries but of many dominant cultures (within or outside the nation state) throughout history and in more recent times the pan-American empire in the post-second World War and post cold war era.

The complacent mainstream society needs to be shaken off its civilisational arrogance and notions of superiority. The irony, however, is that these very specificities of the modern societies and nation states are the ones that the human race is finding itself incapable of living with. Samuel Huntington in The *Clash of Civilizations* warns us that,

"In this new world the most pervasive, important, and dangerous conflicts will not be between social class, rich and poor, or other economically defined groups, but between peoples belonging to different cultural entities. Tribal wars and ethnic conflicts will occur within civilization, violence between states and groups from these civilizations rally to the support of their Kin

countries.... And the most dangerous cultural conflicts are those along the fault lines between civilization"(28).

Huntington too uses the phrase "tribal wars'. This is, however, not a very offensive statement as tribal groups were often at war with each other. But at the same time, throughout history, most of the so called civilised societies and states have been at war with each other. The modern twentieth century alone, despite all its claims of civilisations, scientific temper and understanding, saw killings in war like never before. It is, therefore, problematic to associate wars and conflicts exclusively with the tribal societies as one of their necessary and important characteristics.

In an article called Where it Lives published in the quarterly magazine of the Poetry Society (London) Philip Salom writes:

I discovered poetry, T.S. Eliot and his intellectual and Europeaness and voices, Ted Hughes, whose primal earth energies made immediate sense; then the Americans, starting with Robert Lowell and his musical opposite Wallace Stevens. This was the place for me. Language and memory and the thrill of compressed form. Not nation. Nationalism has never meant much to me. We have seen too much of its obsessions, intensities and as Heaney has written, 'its tribal revenge'. Poetry is the antidote, the other music (7).

Heaney's position, as far as in condemning nationalism for its vindictiveness can be understood and appreciated but in phasing this vindictive nature of nationalism, he should have been more careful than making it sound like an inevitable and natural characteristic of tribal people as if it didn't exist in the modern nation states on their own. This stereotyping of the tribal people in many fields and areas has led the people in general to believe that all that is base and low and disintegrating and hateful is abundantly prevalent among the tribal society. Some might even allow themselves to believe that it has spread to the mainstream civilised society from the tribal people. This helps the hawks in the civilised world to exploit and loot the tribals in many ways and the society in general feel satisfied since they are convicted that it is being done to civilise the hitherto forgotton and backward fellow human beings of the lower ranks and inferior blood.

The uncivilised and seemingly base streaks of tribal behavior, which are prevalent in every society, therefore, need to be identified and interrogated with suitable terminology and new theoretical paradigms with a view to liberate the word 'tribal' from its derogatory connotations.

Who is a Subaltern?

The term 'subaltern', first introduced by the Italian Antonio Gramsci essentially means of lower rank. The word combines the term for 'under' (sub) - 'other' (alter).

The term covers all those classes, groups, castes and those sections and communities in the society who suffer under subjugation and are dominated and exploited by the hegemonic classes and the ruling elite. It is rightly pointed out, "Subaltern studies is about power, who has and who doesn't, who is gaining it and who is losing it. Power is related to representation: which representation have cognitive authority or can secure hegemony, which do not have authority or are not hegemonic" (Beverly 128).

With the passage of time the term subaltern has come to cover a wide range of peoples and classes around the world who have, throughout most part of history been on the receiving end. The 'subaltern' classes could sometimes be difficult to locate since the suppressed, subjugated, exploited, dehumanised and the tortured exist, in many cases, across the barriers of caste, race, colour, gender and political affiliations. In the Indian context subaltern studies have come to be of vital importance for political thinkers, administrators, philosophers, anthropologist, policy makers, and creative writers since many such groups are asserting themselves in socio-political field in the rapidly globalising world.

In the postcolonial context, subaltern studies have found their potent expression. It is in the new found freedom in liberated environment of postcolonial era that such an approach of seeing the 'history from below' and 'history of people will find its true voice, 'History from below' is a concept of historical narrative th social history, which focuses on the perspective of ordinary people, rather than political and other leaders. The term was coined by French historian George Lefebvre (1874-1959) and was popularised by British Marxist historians in the 1960s Thin school of history was among the first to have a sympathetic approach to peasants and working classes. In the colonial age literary texts and other such writings on travels historical and social observations served to be the 'wheels of the empire," "Colonialist literature..... embodied the imperialist point of view.... [it] was informed by theories concerning the superiority of European culture and the rightness of empire" (Boehmer 3).

It was only in the post imperial peroid that various voices rose in the erstwhile colonies which used literary texts to assert their identity not only in relation to the present but to also reveal how distinguished it was before being colonised. As has been pointed out, "Rather than simply being the writing which came after empire, postcolonial literature is generally defined as that which critically or subversively scrutinises the colonial relationship It is writing that sets out in one way or another to resist colonial perspective. decolonization demands symbolic overhaul Postcolonial literature demands that process of overhaul" (Boehmer 3). The literary texts identified as 'postcolonial' question the very paradigm of colonial literature in which the native was romanticised, dehumanised, condemned and simply brushed aside as worthless. In a wider context, it sought to undercut thematically and formally the discourses which supported colonisation classifications, the imagery of subordination.. the myths of power, the race it is also often a nationalist writing. Building on this, postcoloniality can be defined as that condition in which colonized people seek to take their place forcibly or otherwise, as historical agents in an increasingly globalized world (3).

That postcolonialism offers a liberated environment to the hitherto subjugated classes is no exaggeration. It gives an open opportunity to re-read the text and any other form of representation in the new light of the more relaxed socio-political scene. It is a continuous process and continues to offer vast avenues for a cross cultural, historical and political dialogue. Robert Young simplifies the implications of the postcolonial method for the uninitiated:

> *If you are someone who does not identify yourself as western, or as somehow not completely western even though you live in a western country, or someone who is part of a culture and yet excluded by its dominant voices, inside yet outside, then postcolonialism offers you a way of seeing things differently, a language and a politics in which your interests come first, not last. Postcolonialism claims the right of all people on this earth to the same material and cultural well-being. Postcolonialism names a politics and philosophy of activism that contests that disparity, and, so continues in a way the anti-colonial struggle of the past (Young 2003).*

Referring to the tribal population of India, it is imperative to allocate a historical and social location in the wider context of the rest of the Indian nation and society. Throughout history various waves of migration and settlements over the length and breadth of the subcontinent moulded the society into an ever changing entity which rendered it continuous transformation and readjustment as its perpetual features. In a highly competitive and an ever changing social structure, power defined and allocated a place in the society. The tribal society, lesser advanced in terms of technique and sophistication was driven to the borders of the society and colonialism and imperialism (non-European to start with) played decisive roles in this perennial transformation.

Differentiating the two (particularly in the European context), John Mc Leod states:

> *Colonialism is sometimes used interchangeably with 'imperialism', but in truth the terms mean different things. As Peter Childs and Patrick Williams argue, imperialism is an ideological concept which upholds the legitimacy of the economic and military control of one nation by another. Colonialism, however, is only one form of practice which results from the ideology of imperialism, and specifically concerns the settlement of one group of people in a new location. Imperialism is not strictly concerned with the issue of settlement, it does not demand the settlement of different places in order to work (228)*

This study focuses on the tribal as the subaltern in the context of postcolonmal and new historic paradigms. Ever since the widely believed Aryanisation of the Indian peninsula pockets of tribal concentration dwelled all over the country; barring the tribes of north east India, most of the others had some contact with the neighboring peasantry and the town people. They received patronisation from emperors but enjoyed considerable autonomy in their isolated existence in the forests and secluded areas spread all over India.

In the wake of formation of various empires in the subcontinent from time to Nime, those aboriginals who came in contact with the imperial forces were reduced to the status of servants or dasa and the rest escaped into stili deeper and less penetrable forest tracks. The so called mainstream society still considered," the tribal people, though... strange and dangerous," but "were taken for granted as part of the world of hills and forests, and a more or less frictionless coexistence was possible because there was no population pressure, and hence no incentive to deprive the aboriginals off their land. This position persisted during the whole of the Mughal period" (Haimendorf 36) However, things began to change with the advent of the British rule as, ".. a new situation arose the establishment of law and order in outlying areas exposed the aboriginals to the pressure of more advanced populations...traders and money lenders could now establish themselves under the protection of the British administration... by imposing on tribal population, systems of land tenure and revenue collection developed in advanced areas, the government facilitated the transfer of tribal land to members of other ethnic groups" (36).

The tribals, despite their distinguished identity and relative autonomy, remain one of the many subaltern classes in the Indian society. Their territory, the forest, was time and again intruded upon for commercial purposes throughout history. Forests were burnt down in order to clear more land for agriculture and settle their peasants by dominant kingdoms and empires. With the passage of time, the mainstream society's greed for vast forest resources and ther imperial government's forest policies deprived the tribes of their traditional means of livelihood.

In the post-independence period the 'colonisation of the tribal population by the 'native' masters continues. The large scale displacement of the tribal population in order to make way for industrial expansion has disintegrated their social fabric, thrust them into refugee camps, reduced them to the level of bonded labour, drug addiction and prostitution. Talking about the years following the economic liberalisation in India Arundhati Roy notes, "To some these years have brought undreamt of wealth and prosperity, to others such penury, such starvation, such despair as to render them barely human....To the corporations... unimaginable returns on investment. To the adivasis of Dantewada they brought enforced displacement and a brutal, government-sponsored civil war." In an interview to The Times of India, eminent historian Ramachandra Guha observes, "The group that has been most shafted by Indian democracy is tribals. The obvious comparison would be with Dalits and Muslims. The latter are represented in cabinet, you've had presidents and judges. Political parties at least pay lip service to the ideals and aspirations of Dalits and Muslims, but not tribais" (8).

While the discussion about the theory and the practical implications of the subaltern continues, the field is an area of contest between various social term groups and communities. It inevitably brings one to the final question as to who would possibly qualify as a subaltern, and what boundaries of the reality of human existence would fall within the umbrella of subalternity. In this context Kock's analysis of the situation deserves notice:

> *Spivak argues that subaltern in not just a classy word for oppressed, for Other, for somebody who's not getting a piece of the pie.....In postcolonial terms, everything that has limited or no access to the cultural imperialism is subaltern- a space of difference. Now who would say that's just the oppressed? The working class is oppressed. It's not subaltern.... Many people want to claim subalternity. They are the least interesting and the most dangerous. I mean just by being a discriminated-against minority on the university campus, they don't need the word 'subaltern..... They should see what the mechanics of the discrimination are. They're within the hegemonic discourse wanting piece of the pie and not being allowed, so let them speak, use the hegemonic discourse. They should not call themselves subaltern (Kock 29).*

Making clear the demarcation between history and literature, in terms of subaltern discourse, Spivak warns, "Those who read or write literature can claim as little of subaltern status as those who read or write history. The difference is that the subaltern as object is supposed to be imagined in one case and real in another. I am suggesting that it is a bit of both in both cases. The writer acknowledges this by claiming to do reserach (my fiction is also historical), The historian might acknowledge this by looking at the mechanics of representation- my history is also fictive" (Spivak 1987:95).

In the case of the Indian sub-continent, the project to undertake 'subaltern studies' as 'Writings on South Asian History and Society' was initiated in the early nineteen eighties with Ranajit Guha as the editor. The aim of the studies was to 'get rid of the elitism of colonialist, nationalist and Marxist historiographies', which, according to [Guha], uniformly represented popular resistance against the colonial order and the freedom struggle generally as resulting from a process of mobilisation from the top (Pouchepadass 101). The subaltern studies carried out thus far has attempted, quite successfully, to bring to the fore the almost forgotten, or at best, neglected sagas of the common people's participation in not just the national freedom struggle but also for the restoration of their rights and dignity and their own lives without any leader from the mainstream society. Most of these protests and insurgencies were led by the so-called downtrodden masses all by themselves. This initiative tries to unearth numerous such instances from throughout the length and breadth of the country, across the past more than two centuries.

The hitherto successful, though often challenged, claim of the colonialists and the nationalists to monopolise the struggle for independence and the general emancipation of the pan-Indian issues have been put to severe tests by the initiative. Ranajit Guha categorically declared at the very onset of the Subaltern Studies initiative:

> *The historiography of Indian nationalism has for a long time been dominated by elitism- colonialist elitism and bourgeois- nationalist elitism. Both originated as the ideological product of British rule in India... Both these varieties of elitism share the prejudice that the making of the Indian nation and the development of the consciousness nationalism- which informed this process, were exclusively or predominately elite achievements. In the colonialist and neo-colonialist historiographies these achievements are credited to British colonial rulers, administrators, policies, institutions and culture; in the nationalist and neo-nationalist writings to Indian elite personalities, institutions, activities and ideas (Guha 1982: 1).*

What these studies attempted to highlight was the 'inadequacy' of such 'elitist historiography' which followed directly from the 'narrow and partial view of politics' which Guha mentions are because of the class outlook' of the actors and the writers of these historiographies. The deliberate attempt to sideline the contribution of the less privileged class is rooted in the, ".. contradiction that the elite faced it had to speak in the name of the masses if it wanted to stand a chance in the confrontation with the colonial power, but it feared, and contained with difficulty, the irrepressible autonomy of their modes of protest... [therefore] the main aim of the project was not to propose a new (and rather simplistic) model of social stratification, but to reinstate power as a crucial dimension of social organisation, and to demonstrate that the liberal bourgeois conception of the nation-states as a plural but the consensual entity is fundamentally false" (Pouchepadass 117).

Ranajit Guha also points out how such writings on history fail to render a clear explanation of our nationalism because:

> *...it fails to acknowledge, far less interpret, the contribution made by the people on their own, that is, independently of the elite to the making and development of this nationalism. In this particular respect the poverty of this historiography is demonstrated beyond doubt by its failure to undetstand and assess the mass articulation of this nationalism except, negatively, as a law and order problem, and positively, if at all, either as a response to the charisma of certain elite leaders or in the currently more fashionable terms of vertical mobilization by the manipulation of factions (Guha 1982: 3).*

One of the greatest impacts of the subaltern study has been the widespread interest this effort has generated among the scholars and students of not only history and sociology but even literature. The revelations of hidden facts of history have not just come to light through the historical research but even through literature. The numerous sagas of the freedom movements that had been buried beneath layers of biased historiographies have come to light through various voices without which the story of our past would have been poorer for the people would not have been able to appreciate the effort of those who had been "...condescendingly marginalised. Only in the past decade... historians of India rediscovered the tremendous variety of local resistance of subaltern groups to their particular conditions of oppression and their corresponding vision of the good life" (Dasgupta 101). Drawing attention to the various uprisings led by the tribal heroes Dasgupta writes, "The histories of the Hul of 1855, the Birsa Munda uprising and the Eka movement, to name but a few, have brought to the fore alternative traditions of Indian politics- ones which consciously or implicitly challenge the notion of an unitary domain of politics in South Asian societies and the appropriation of all politics by the elite" (101)

Literature and other types of written documents prove to be of great usage in establishing 'people' at the centre of the public domain. This medium has been put to optimum use by authors, journalists and social activists to mould social reality as perceived by them into written documents of various hues. Since these documents, particularly in the form of novels, command legitimacy and are seen as genuine portrayal of reality, they come to perform the role of the prism through which crtitics view the society at large. As Jacques Pouchepadass remarks:

> *...an increasing use is made of literary sources. Textual criticism, it must be remembered, was one of the methods of enquiry advocated and used by Ranajit Guha from the very beginning. Moreover, the departments of literary studies of American universities are among the most active centres of dissemination of the type of epistemological questionings which now inspire the authors of the series (not only Edward Said but also Gayatri Spivak,... belong to this academic sphere) (120).*

Subaltern studies thus mark a shift in focus from the hegemonic classes or focus to the marginalized ones and this could be illustrated, for instance from the Oriya classic of Gopinath Mohanty *Matimataal*. The protagonist, Ravi, though from the hegemonic landlord class is a 'sosialist at heart. He believes in and strives for classless society and rises in a quiet rebellion beginning at home. Earlier in his school days he would ponder over the futility of so much that was being taught. While in school he felt that the British rule was embarrassing and humiliating and now to continue to learn English language was slavish since it legitimised the victory of the empire. The protagonist Ravi wonders, "Why just English, there were many other lessons that he thought were unnecessary. History for instance, numerous kings, countless wars, dates and events cramming them caused headaches. From Alfred to Aurangzeb" (Mohanty 96).

He often felt those to be the tales of high and mighty: "Where did the poor stand admist all that? History talks about the kings and rulers of all ages but what about the whereabouts of the rest of the people?" (96).

Once during the lessons of the Maurya dynasty he asked about the festivals and customs of the common villagers. About the sweets and delicacies they made. All laughed at this simpleton. The teacher thought it to be a prank. He was rebuked (97).

Ravi's attitude calls out for the imperative need to shift the focus from the top to the bottom on the common people and the commonplace things. He tries to engage others in a discussion on the way people lived in those ages instead of merely the kings, rulers, wars, coronations, events and all the intrigues of which young minds are flooded with and forced to cram. This is virtually the field and focus of the subaltern studies. In this discipline it's the common man from whose perspective things and issues are attempted to be seen. The subaltern collective in *Matimataal* is the simplified subaltern discourse in the language of the subaltern.

The idea of shifting of this focus is at the centre of the soul of the subaltern studies not for the sake of an undue mass crediting of the larger sections of the society but to reverse the order of the mainstream attitude to give the masses their due. It finds an echo in what Ranajit Guha was to criticise many years after the publication of the said novel. Guha laments the role that the current historiography plays in downplaying the role played by the subaltern groups all over the land as far the modern nationalism in India is concerned. Guha is categorical in stating:

> *What is clearly left out of this un-historical historiography is the politics of the people. For parallel to the domain of elite politics there existed throughout the colonial period another domain of Indian politics in which the principal actors were not the dominant groups of the indigenous society or the colonial authorities but the subaltern classes and groups constituting the masses of the labouring population and the intermediate strata in town and country- that is, the people. This was an autonomous domain, for it neither originated from elite politics nor did its existence depend on the latter (1982: 4).*

In a short story titled *A Reader* by the Russian writer Maxim Gorky, the narrator, one night meets an unusual man in the strect. The observations or the demands made by the unusual man, who comes to represent the common reader, that an author is expected to cater to the needs of the common man. Would qualify for the contemporary subaltern concerns and priorities. The man makes the author acquainted with his observations about the role he ought to play. This observation, to an extent, underlines the power of fiction (or therby literature in general) and therefore its utility for the study of representation of the subaltern in various media in the society. The observation made by the 'reader' emphasizes this role vis-a vis the 'duties' of an author

> *It is essential that human beings laugh after all, this ability is one of the few things that distinguish men from animals. Can you call forth any laughter but that of censure, cheap laughter at the expense of human beings who are funny only because they are pitable? Try to understand that your right to preach must spring from an ability to awaken sincere sentiments which, like hammers, must knock down and destroy old confining forms of life so that roomier ones may be built up (274).*

The choice of fictional works for this study is foregrounded in the popularity and accessibility of this genre. Through the creative medium of the novel the study aims to awaken and deepen human sensibility towards the marginalized, deprived and voiceless sections of human society. They are offered a fictional voice. The 'authenticity' of a fictional voice can not be undermined for most of the socially aware authors haven't distorted their subject matter except that they have been pitched in a fictional setting. Theresa M. Senft writes,

> *...not wishing to be herself "part of the problem", Spivak uses her international academic/ clout in order to read and critique Mahasweta's story, Douloti the Beautiful. Douloti is the daughter of a tribal bonded worker in rural India. Douloti in the course of the story is abducted by an upper*

caste (non-tribal) India and sold into bonded prostitution. It is from the fictional world of Douloti that Spivak begins her field report, informing her international readership that Douloti's tale, while a fiction, could very well be real (Senft 275).

It is primarily fiction that gave the author plenty of room and options to not just record the socio-economic trends of the society but portray the lives of life-like characters for whom such trends provided not just the background but the very truth of their existence. Bhasha fiction comes closer to the 'reality' of their subjects.

From Fakir Mohan Senapati to Mahasweta Devi; through Premchand, Gopinath Mohanty, Shivaji Sawant, Pratibha Ray, Mahadevi Verma, Nirmal Verma, Krishna Sobti and Lakshman Gaekwad, to name just a few, bhasha literature captures the compelling reality and desperate existence of not just the characters but even the socio-economic conditions that form background against which they are pitted Spivak upholds the rationale of fiction and its role in forming the collective expression of the society since, history tells us what happened and fiction what may have happened and indeed may happen (333).

According to Dr. Gyaneshwar Mishra, novel writing started in India as a result of the Indian author's exposure to Western literature, from mid-nineteenth century onward. Fakir Mohan Senapati (1843-1918) is the first major novelist whose Chha Mana Atha Guntha (Six Acres and Thirty Two Decimals, 1897), dealing with the exploitation of the peasants by a Zamindar, is a landmark in Indian literature. Senapati wrote in the tradition of realism, about ordinary men and women and their problems. Explaining the background to the pathbreaking novel, Mayadhar Mansinha notes:

The British came to Orissa in 1803....due to the ruthless measures turned overnight thousands of gentlemen-farmers into beggars. Cowri, the traditional common currency of Orissa was forbidden thousands of farmers lost their ancestral lands due to their inability to pay taxes in the new currency...and the notorious sunset law...enabled even clerks in Calcutta to become owners of historic estates in Orissa... Fakirmohan's novel deals with this sad phase...spanning the fust fifty years of British rule in India (61).

Regional literature, fiction in particular, is marked by the representation and voice that the aspiration of the masses find in it. Novels written between late twenties and forties are fired with nationalism. Many other concerns of the vast multitudes of people are voiced in regional fiction, such as the condition of the peasants, marginalised section of the society without any romanticisation of the subjects. Returning to Fakirmohan's classic pioneering novel is inevitalbe since it is one of those novels that voiced the contemporary concern of the subjugated in India, though in a local setting of Orissa but something which echoed all over the land:

Oh ye humble herons of India, see how the English cormorants fly across distant seas to our land and return gleefully, with their erstwhile empty pockets filled with excellent fish, while you fools, who live on the boughs of trees standing close to this tank, fail to get more than a few of the small fry after hard day-long struggles. A bitter war of existence is on now You may expect more and more cormorants flying thither very soon. They might eat all the fish in the tank. If you are keen on your own survival, you had better behave like those cormorants. You have to learn how to swim the seas. I do not know else, in future, you could even keep body and soul together (63- 4).

Many such examples of fiction are available throughout the freedom movement and thereafter, through literary voices of Bankimchandra, Premchand, Mahasweta Devi, Gopinath Mohanty and, more recently, Lakshman Gaekwad. It is, therefore, through the creative medium of fiction that this study aims to enhance its understanding of the tribal people of India whom Nehru thought "...the civilised world had much to learn from an extremely disciplined people, often a great deal more democratic than most others in India. Above all they are a people who sing and dance and try to enjoy life, not people who sit in stock exchange, shout at one another and think themselves civilized" (Ramchandra Guha 269).

It is extraordinary that Verrier Elwin, of all the anthropologists and ethnographers, should have sensed what was in store for the tribals even after the country gained independence. That was precisely why he was almost always in confrontation with sociologists such as G. S. Ghurye who advocated 'integrationist' plans for the tribals with the rest of the Indian society, as opposed to his [Elwin's] 'protectionist approach (Deshpande 39) Elwin was exceptional in the sense that he lived among the people he often wrote about and fought for. His literature too was inspired by his concern for the tribal society as "all his books were written in the hope that they might help forestall, or at least delay, the degradation and exploitation of the tribes. Elwin hoped his books might help protect the aboriginal from some of the deadly shafts of exploitation, interference and repression that civilisation so constantly launches at his heart" (Ramchandra Guha 339).

This study aims to closely examine in a great detail the manner in which the tribal population of India is represented in its fiction. This fiction is selected from regional languages such as Marathi, Bengali, Oriya as well as English. Some of these authors have had first hand experience of living with the subject of their fictional narratives and some have depended more on their imagination and information. The portrayal of the tribals through this wide range of literature, not only in terms of geographical space but even through many cultures and languages.

The authors and their works included in this book include Mahasweta Devi's *Aranyer Adhikar* (1977), Shivaji Sawant's *Mrityunjay* (1974), Pratibha Ray's *Aadibhoomi* (1993), Gopinath Mohanty's *Paraja* (1945) and *Maatimataal* (1964), and Arun Joshi's *The Strange Case of Billy Biswas* (1971).

Mahashweta Devi was born in a middle class family in Dacca (now the capital of Bangladesh) in 1926. The family moved to India in 1947. She later passed M.A. in English and began teaching literature in 1964. She believes in the power of the common man and in the fact that the real history is made by ordinary people. She acknowledges the reason and the inspiration for her writing to be those people who are exploited and used, and yet don't accept defeat. Aranyer Adhikar (The Rights of the Forests) is based on the life of Birsa Munda, a tribal rebel from Chhotanagpur. Caught between the twin perspectives of the British officials and the Birsaites (his cult followers), the true portrayal of the real Birsa Munda has always been a challenge for anyone.

Mahashweta Devi, through her fiction, tries to do full justice to the representation of the character and struggle of Birsa Munda and his people, in keeping up with her philosophy that a creative writer should have a social conscience. The novel also throws light on the plight of the tribal people who find themselves being deprived of one thing after another by the colonial regime and who, Mahasweta believes, continue to suffer as the rest of India continues to develop. Many of her other writings, such as Chotti Munda evam Tar Tir (1980), deal with issues related to the lives and sufferings of the tribals from Bihar, Madhya Pradesh, Chhattisgarh and Bengal who have been facing oppression at the hands of the British officials, landlords and government officials in independent India.

Shivaji Sawant is one of the finest Marathi novelists. He was born in Kolhapur in Maharashtra and rose to eminence in the field of literature. He served as a teacher for many decades. He later joined as the editor of Maharashtra education department's magazine Lokshikshan Sawant's major novels include *Mrityunjay*, *Chhaya*, *Yugandhara* and *Purushottamnama*. Although recognized as a historical writer, his works are known for strong political undertones that underline and question the very power structures of the society. *Mrityunjay* (The Death Conqueror), published in 1974, is a stunning narrative of the life of the sidelined Mahabharata hero Karna. The novel deals in detail (nine sections) with the anguish of the the protagonist about his life long struggle against a system of power that should have bowed to his valour but instead humiliated him merely because he belonged to a humble background. It's an exercise in extending the limits of subalternity beyond its accepted boundaries.

Gopinath Mohanty was born in Nagabali in Orissa in 1914. He completed his M.A. from Patna University in 1936. He joined the Orissa Administrative Services in 1938 and served among the tribals in Koraput districts. This was the beginning of his experiences of the people who would be the subjects of the most of his fiction. His first novel *Mana Gahirara Chasa* (1940) was followed by many of his prominent novels such as *Paraja* (1945), *Amrutara Santan* (1947) and *Matimataal* (1964). His novels deal with the portrayal of the tribals in particular. Paraja is a moving tale of a family belonging to the Paraja tribe who were first exploited and subsequently ruined at the hands of a petty forest guard and the money lender. Matimataal, though subtly deals with the love story of Ravi and Chhavi, it draws a real picture of the lives of those who are at the lower step of the social ladder and their struggle for re-defining the power paradigm that is repeatedly questioned from a subaltern point of view.

Pratibha Ray, the widely renowned Oriya novelist, was born in Cuttack (Grissa) in 1943. Her first novel Barsha Basanta Baishakha was published in 1974. Her Post-Doctoral thesis Tribalism and Criminology of Bonda Highlander focuses on Bonda tribe, which is one of most backward tribes of Orissa, and it is the Bonda tribe on which her novel Adibhoomi is based. Her literary craft is shaped by her philosophy of life which is based on social equality, that is, a society that has no distinction based on caste, religion, sex and status. She is a versatile writer and some of her novels are *Aranya* (1977), *Ashabari* (1980), and *Yajnaseni* (1984). Yajnaseni. The Story of Draupadi, originally published in Oriya in 1984 and then translated into English in 1995 by Pradip Bhattacharya, is an example of the postcolonial consciousness which considers the tribal question with a sense of being on equal terms with each other. Based on the life of Draupadi, against the background of Mahabharata, it re-tells the tale of possibly the central female character of the epic. The novel *Adibhoomi* (1993), which is a part of the current study offers a detailed account of the life of Bonda tribe. Strangely enough the Bonda people living on the hills just know that they belong to the 'Remo caste', i.e., the human beings However, they are in constant confrontation not only amongst themselves but also with those non-Bondas living in the lower areas. Although the novel is devoid of any coherent plot or characterization, it is rich in recording the way of life of the Bonda tribe and captures their social reality like a social historian.

Arun Joshi was born in 1939 in Varanasi. He received his higher education in the USA and returned to India as an industrial manager. Some of his novels are *The Foreigner*, *The City and the River*, and *The Last Labyrinth* for which he was awarded the Sahitya Akademi Award in 1982. Joshi's *The Strange Case of Billy Biswas* was published in 1971. It is a compelling story of the protagonist Bimal Biswas who has almost everything that one can ask for in the centre of metropolitan Delhi. Fed up with civilization and possessed by extraordinary obsession he disappears into the forests of central India to live among the tribals there, in search of a new life, a meaning and possibly truth itself The novel offers a critique of life and civilization as we understand it. The novel portrays a couple of tribal characters who play a pivotal role in the second life of Billy Biswas.

Most of these narratives were written after India attained its freedom and when the soul of a nation, long suppressed, finds utterance. This observation by Nehru sets the tone of this study but ironically when we talk about India, the nation per se, it becomes imperative to ask, which India? The India that had been suppressed by the imperial Britain or those numerous Indias that have been suppressed for far too long by the hegemonic classes and castes within the nation? And whose voice? The voice for the entire sub-continent that rose in unison against the western dominance, even though some are yet to be given due acknowledgement, or those unheard voices that have been since the Vedic times, craftily mentioned of as evil 'Rakshashas' of the dark forests (Thapar 56), and later thought of to be of the 'bogey men with which mothers frightened their naughty children' (Basham 198).

Commenting on how fiction sometimes comes to represent reality, not just of the present time but even historical in nature, Spivak writes (in this case about Mahasweta Devi's *Aranyer Adhikar*, 1977) "...the prose is beginning to bend into full-fledged 'historical fiction', history imagined into fiction. The division between fact (historical event) and fiction (literary event) is operative in all these moves. Indeed, her repeated claim to legitimacy is that she researches thoroughly everything she represents in fiction. Fiction of this sort relies for its effect on its effects of the real" (95). Here one finds the literary activity wedded to the larger social cause which takes us back to Gorky's 'reader' who would like literature to focus on the ability to awaken sincere sentiments' to 'knock down and destroy old confining forms of life, hatred of human shortcomings and a great love for the common man a love born of his sufferings.

The study, therefore, attempts to recognise the foundation of life and reality of the tribal world. Recognising literary fiction as a genuine medium of dialogue in modern society, the current thesis undertakes the re-examination of the above mentioned texts to interrogate them in the context of contemporary socio-political reality and the polemics of representation.

Works Cited:

Amin, Shahid "Approver's Testimony, Judicial Discourse. The Case of Chauri Chaura" 1987. Subaltern Studies. Ed. Ranajit Guha. 2nd ed. Vol. V. New Delhi: Oxford UP, 1995. Print.

Balfour, Edward G., ed. Enclopedia Asiatica Comprising Indian Subcontinent Eastern and Southern Asia. Commercial, Industrial and Scientific, 1858. 3rd ed. Vol 5. New New Delhi: Cosmo, 1976. Print. 9 vols.

Basham, A.L. The Wonder That Was India. 1967. 3rd ed. New Delhi: Rupa, 1997. Print.

Beverly, John. Subalternity and Representation Arguments in Cultural Theory Durham: Duke University Press, 1999. Google Book Search. Web.

Bochmer, Elleke, Colonial and Postcolonial Literature. 1995. New Delhi: OUP, 2006: Print.

Bowil, Andrew. Aesthetics and Subjectivity: From Kant to Nietzsche. Manchester:

Manchester UP, 1990. Google Book Search. Web. 20 December 2010.

Chanda, Nayan. Bound Together How Traders, Preachers, Adventurers, and Warriors Preached Globalization. Penguin, 2007. Print.

Chatterjee, Roma. "The Nationalist Sociology of Benoy Kumar Sarkar" (106-131) Anthropology in the East Founders of Indian Sociology and Anthropology. Eds. Patricia Uberoi et al. Ranikhet: Permanent Black, 2007. Print.

Dasgupta, Sangeeta. "Recasting the Oraons and the 'Tribe' Sarat Chandra Roy's Anthology (132-171) Anthropology in the East. Founders of Indian Sociology and Anthropology. Eds. Patricia Uberoi et al. Ranikhet. Permanent Black, 2007. Print.

Dasgupta, Swapan "Adivasi Politics in Midnapore, c. 1760-1924" (101-135), 1985. Subaltern Studies. Ed. Ranajit Guha. Vol. IV. New Delhi: Oxford UP, 2005. Print.

Deshpande, Satish, Patricia Uberoi and Nandini Sunder, eds. Introduction. Anthropology in the East: Founders of Indian Sociology and Anthropology. Ranikhet: Permanent Black, 2007, Print

Ferguson, Niall. Empire: How Britain Made the Modern World. 2003. New Delhi: Penguin, 2008. Print.

Frantz, Fanon. The Wretched of the Earth: A Negro Psychoanalyst's Study of the Problems of Racism and Colonialism in the World Today. 1961. Trans. Constance Farrington, New York: Penguin, 2001. Google Book Search. Web. 12 May 2009.

Foucoult, Michel. Discipline and Punish The Birth of the Prison 1975. Trans. Alan Sheridan. New York: Vintage Books, 1995. Google Book Search. Web. 12 May 2009

Gibbon, Edward. The Decline and Fall of the Roman Empire. 1776-1788. Ed. Antony Lentin and Brian Norman. London: Wordsworth, 1998. Print.

Gorky, Maxim. Selected Short Stories. New Delhi: Crest Publishing Home, 2003. Print.

Guha, Ramchandra. "Between Anthropology and Literature: The Ethnography of Verrier Elwin" (330-359). Anthropology in the East: Founders of Indian Sociology and Anthropology. Eds. Patricia Uberoi et al. Ranikhet: Permanent Black, 2007. Print.

_ _ _ _. India After Gandhi: The History of the World's Largest Democracy. London. Picador, 2007. Print.

_ _ _ _. Interview, New Delhi: The Times of India, 11 May, 2007.

Guha, Ranajit. "The Prose of Counter- Insurgency." 1983. Subaltern Studies. Ed Ranajit Guha. 2nd ed. Vol. II. New Delhi: Oxford UP, 1995. Print.

Haimendorf, Christoph von furer. Tribes of India. The Struggle for Survival, New Delhi: OUP, 1982. Print.

Huntington, Samuel. The Clash of Civilizations, 1996. New Delhi: Penguin, 1997. Print.

Kipling, Rudyard. Stories of India. Ed. Sudhakar Marathe. New Delhi: Penguin, 2003. Print.

Kock, Leon. "Interview With Gayatri Chakravorty Spivak: New Nation Writer's Conference in South Africa." A Review of International English Literature. 23(3) 1992 pp. 29-47. Google Book Search. Web. 11 May, 2011

Mansinha, Mayadhar Fakir Mohan Senapati Makers of Indian Literature.1976. New Delhi: Sahitya Akademi, 1997. Print.

Marathe, Sudhakar. Introduction. Stories of India. By Rudyard Kipling. Ed. Marathe. New Delhi: Penguin, 2003. Print.

Mitchell, W. "Representation." Critical Terms for Literary Study Eds. F Lentricchia and T Mc Laughlin. 2nd ed. Chicago: University of Chicago Press, 1995. Print

Mohanty, Gopinath Maatimataal, 1964. Trans. Shankarlal Purohit. New Delhi Jnanpith, 2001. Print.

Muller, F. Max. India: What Can it Teach Us? New Delhi: Rupa, 2002. Print.

Nehru, Jawaharlal. "Tryst With Destiny." Speech on the Granting of Indian Independence, August 14, 1947. Penguin Book of Twentieth Century Speeches. Ed. Brian Mac Arthur. London: Penguin/ Viking, 1992. Pp. 234- 237. Print.

New York Times. Wild Tribes of India Becoming Civilized: Lord Curzon's Trip Through Remote Districts. December 22, 1901. Google Book Search. Web. 30 June 2008

Pouchepadass, Jacques. "Subaltern Studies as Post-Colonial Critique of Modernity." Remapping Knowledge: The Making of South Asian Studies in India, Europe and America (19-20th Centuries). New Delhi: Three Essays Collective, 2004. Print

Ray, Niharranjan. Introduction The Tribal Situation in India, 1972. Ed. K. Suresh Singh. Shimla Indian Institute of Advanced Study, 2002. Print.

Roy, Arundhati. The Shape of the Beast: Conversation with Arundhati Roy. Penguin Viking, 2008). R.Rangachari et al, Large Dams: India's Experience, 2000, World Commission on Dams (WCD) case study prepared as an input to the World Commission on Dams, Cape town, online at http://www.dams.org/Docs/ kbase/studies/csinnain.pdf.

Said, Edward W. Culture and Imperialism. 1993. New York: Vintage, 1994. Print.

Salmon, Philip. "Where It Lives." Poetry Society Quaterly. London, 2001. Print.

Shaughnessy, M. and J.Stadler. Media and Society: An Introduction. 3rd ed. South Melbourne: OUP, 2006. Print.

Senft, Theresa M. Writing (and) Independence: Gayatri Spivak and the Dark Comments of Feminine, originally appeared in women and performance, Vol. 7. No.2, Issue 14-15, Spring 1995, pp 275-286. Google Book Search. Web. 12 May 2009.

Sills, David. ed International Encyclopedia of the Social Sciences. New York Macmillan// Free Press, 1968. Vol. 16 (p. 146-151). Print.

Singh, Pankaj K., ed. The Politics of Literary Theory and Representation: Writings on

Activism and Aesthetics. New Delhi: Manohar Publications, 2003. Print.

Solomon, Robert C. "Subjectivity", Oxford Companion to Philosophy, OU P, 2005. Google Book Search. Web. 30 August 2008.

Spivak, Gayatri Chakravorty. "A Literary Representation of the Subaltern: Mahasweta Devi's 'Stanadayini'" (91-134). 1987. Subaltern Studies. Ed. Ranajit Guha. 2nd ed. Vol. V. New Delhi: OUP, 1995. Print.

_ _ _ _. "Discussion: An Afterword on the New Subaltern" (305-335), 2000. Subaltern Studies: Community, Gender and Violence. Eds. Pariha Chatterjee and Pradeep Jeganathan. Vol. XI. New Delhi: Permanent Black, 2009. Print.

Thapar, Romila. Early India: From the Origins to AD 1300. New Delhi: Penguin, 2002. Print.

Tulasidas, Goswami. Shri Ramacharitamanasa: The Holy Lake of the Acts of Lord Rama Gorakhpur (UP, India): Gita Press, 2004.

Young, Robert J. C. Postcolonialism: A Very Short Introduction, New York: OUP. 2003. Print.

Chapter - 2

Historical Representation of Caste, Tribe & the Subaltern

Representation in its entirety has been a perennial problem through cultures, societies and nations. In general, representation is defined by the Oxford Dictionary as: 'The act of presenting somebody or something in a particular way, something that shows or describes something (1296). In a technical context the dictionary defines this act as "(especially of a style of art or painting) trying to show things as they really are." Dictionary definitions affirm the nature of representation as it truly ought to be, ranging from speaking on someone's behalf to depicting someone in art, dance, literature or in any other form. However, when it comes to the reality it becomes a tool in the hands of the representer who intentionally or otherwise uses it to purposes that have lasting results. Therefore, the act of representation ends up being frought with bias, stemming out of reasons based on personal views or allegiance to a point of view since, despite the fact of representation being the reproduction/representation of a likeness, these representations are most often thought to be somewhat realistic, a clear image of the represented object and this is why it becomes imperative to constantly question representations. If there is always an element of interpretation involved in representation, we must then note who may be doing the interpreting" (Dimri 64).

The mechanism of representation in literary narratives, as in most other areas, involves three parts: The representer, the represented and the observer (reader, consumer, viewer, listener, spectator etc). It is the problematic functioning of this this mechanism that the subaltern approach to literary criticism aims to 'mend' or at the least dissect and discuss. This approach may draw its origin from antiquity itself as Jaiwantı Dimri has argued that since antiquity, representation has played a decisive role in understanding the primary knowledge systems of literature, aesthetics and semiotics. The critical theories of Plato and Aristotle had taken cognizance of the correlation between representation and literature. Plato's theory of mimesis, as is common knowledge, is foregrounded in representation and as for Aristotle, he considered each mode of representation verbal, visual or musical- as natural to human beings since mimesis is a natural instinct in man. As opposed to Aristotle, Plato looked at representation with more caution since he perceived representation as an intervening agency between the viewer and the real which create illusions so as to lead one away from real things. Consequently, Plato had expressed the need to control and monitor representation a fact that is forcefully reiterated in the modern postcolonial, feminist and subaltern discourse.

In most cases the attitude of the representer towards the subject of representation (or the represented) also depends on the relationship between the two or the positions that both occupy in the social set up. The entire act of representation in literary narratives or other forms is thus subject to the 'distance between the representer and the represented. This representing distance determines the approach of the representer towards the represented. Reasons for this distance could be socio- historical where the subject is the other" In this sense the representer and the represented could be locked in a rather hegemonic relationship where the already elastic situation is generally stretched, resulting in arrogance, bias and suspicion towards the subject of representation. However, this distance could be contracted or roduced mentally by considering a point of view which could be initiated by compassion (not necessarily sympathy) and must finally rest on the sense of justice towards the subject.

A just case in point is that of Sharat Chander Roy, the anthropologist who made valuable contribution to the study of aboriginal tribes of Chhotanagpur and its surrounding areas during the first half of the twentieth century. During his initial years as an anthropologist, Roy possibly saw himself as the righteous imperial agent who condescended upon the subject of his observation. Sangeeta Dasgupta has rightly pointed out that,

> *...between the publication of The Mundas and Their Country in 1912 and The Oraons of Chotanagpur in 1915, and The Aborigines of Chotanagpur Their Proper Status in the Reformed Constitution in 1936, Sharat Chander Roy went through a complete change that marked the shift in his attitude towards his subjects of study. It was the*

image of the 'primitive savage that Roy wished to reverse in these articles The anthropologist, who had earlier condemned the "aborigines' as 'primitive', and their culture as 'rude' and 'backward'. now reversed his stance: "Perhaps the hypnotic suggestion of the inappropriate term "primitive" sometimes loosely applied to them, is responsible for the illusion that the Chotanagpur aborigines are still savages who should be regarded as a standing menace to peace and good governance. As far as the principle aboriginal tribes of Chotanagpur - the Mundas, Hos and Bhumijes- they too possess a culture of their own which is not insignificant or of a mean order (158).

This attitudinal shift in the approach of Sharat Chander Roy is what is intended by the 'contracting' or 'reducing the distance between the representer and the represented. What began with Roy as an almost hegemonic approach by someone from an exalted position was subsequently fine tuned compassion and then purged' by a fine sense of justice towards his subjects the aborigines of Chotanagpur, a change over a space of two decades that was 'informed by a detailed study and keen observation instead of gross generalizations of an uninterested outsider that he indulged in, in his earlier writings on the subject.

A stunning example that one may mention here would be a comparative study of the great Anglo Indian writer Rudyard Kipling's two stories in terms of the representation of the natives and his own' people, the

Anglo- Indians. The short stories are *Lispeth* and *At The Pit's Mouth.*

Lispeth is about a hill girl adopted, converted and brought up by the missionaries at Kotgarh and who had been christened Elizabeth but was known as Lispeth as per the pahari pronunciation. It is a story of a girl who had, for the first seventeen years of her life, lived at the missionary and learnt their customs till she falls in love at the first sight' with an English traveler whom she helped bring to the missionary after he had fallen unconscious on the way. Unwittingly though Lispeth introduces him to the Chaplain's wife as, "This is my husband I found him on the Bagi road. He has hurt himself. We will nurse him, and when he is well your husband shall marry him to me" (Kipling 10). The story is punctuated by gross and derogatory generalization of the natives by Kipling Kipling is callous and his racist attitude is both implicit and explicit Describing her feelings for the Englishman, Kipling writes, "Being a savage by birth, she took no trouble to hide her feelings, and the Englishman was amused" (11). Towards the end of the short story Kipling gives his own views on the life of Lispeth after she left the Kotgarh mission. Kipling writes: "She took to her own unclean people savagely, as if to make up the arrears of the life she had stepped out of, and, in a little time, she married a wood-cutter who beat her after the manner of paharis, and her beauty faded soon" (13). Fading of her beauty is clearly understandable but the gross generalization of the people being 'unclean' and Lispeth being beaten by her husband 'after the manner of the paharis' betrays the racial attitude of the author who, it could be said, was writing about the subject from a very comfortable distance and his understanding of the subjects was limited and clouded, very possibly by the colonial setting of the the ruler and the ruled. Therefore the distance between the presenter and the presented, which may be attributed to the colonial setting that both are parts of, results in providing the author room enough for generalization and undermining statements Gyanendra Pandey righily observes, "British colonialism in India regularly represented the 'native' as the primitive Other, and violence- and, at other times, its exact opposite, complete passivity- as his history ('her' being subsumed in "his')" (2005 195).

The second story in sharp contrast is At *The Pit's Mouth* which is entirely about the European community in Sımia. It is about a 'Man and his Wife and a Tertium Quid' (88) Both *Lispeth* and *At The Pit's Mouth* are marked by a stark absence of names of any Europeans with a sole exception of the Tertium Quid who, at a couple of places we hear being addressed Frank by the Man's Wife. All the other European characters are otherwise mentioned as the Chaplain, the Chaplain's wife, the Englishman, the Man and the Man's Wife.

The story is about an Englishwoman who had been accommodated at Sımla at eight hundred and fifty rupees a month by her Englishman husband who toiled in the heat of the Indian plains at merely two hundred rupees at month. The Wife, as Kipling mentions the woman, flirted at Simla with a bachelor Englishman described by the author as a Tertuum Quid. Towards the end of the story the Tertium Quid slides and tumbles down the gorge upon his horse as both of them were riding along the Himalayan-Tibet Road, just a couple of minutes after the Man's Wife had merrily declared "Now we are going to Tibet and to which the Tertium Quid had as merrily replied, "Into Tibet, ever so far from people who say horrid things, and hubbies who write stupid letters. With you- to the end of the world' (92). The Tertium Quid was found dead nine hundrd feet below in a field of corn and the Man's Wife remained temporarily insane and in bed for a few days so much so that she could not attend Frank's funeral.

What seems to be intriguing, though quite natural for Kipling's writing is that he does not generalise the infidelity of the Man's Wife as typical of the Europeans in India or Englishwomen in Simla or the ones that lived in Simla while their husbands toiled in military regiments or attended to business in the hot plains. The Man's Wife is just one character and that is how it ought to be. It may safely be said that it was Kipling's racial allegiance to his own people that possibly prevented him from making general statements about his own people based on an erring wife, whose name is not mentioned. Kipling did advocate water tight compartments for various races in his wrtings as the opening lines of his another short story "Beyond The Pale' suggest, "A man should, whatever happens, keep to his own caste, race, and breed. Let the White go to the White and the Black to the Black. Then whatever trouble falls is in the ordinary course of things- neither sudden, alien, nor expected" (33).

This tendency of representing the 'inferior other' or the ruled races' is reflected in Lispeth and is to found nowhere in At The Pit's Mouth. This tendency is contextualised through Dimri's observations, "Foregrounded on the assumption that a subaltern can stand in for other subalterns, the mass media tends to take representations of the subaltern as allegorical Since representations of the marginalised are few, the few available are thought to be representative of all marginalised peoples. The few images are thought to be typical, sometimes not only of members of a particular minority group, but of all minorities in general" (Dimri 67).

In addition to not generalising, Kipling also refuses to let anyone know more about the relationship between the Man's Wife and the Tertium Quid He states, "I decline to state positively whether there was anything uretrievably wrong in the relations between the Man's Wife and the Tertium Quid. If there was, and hereon you must form your own opinion, it was the Man's Wife's fault" (89) The only generalisation Kipling indulges in is about Sımla Simla is a strange place and its customs are peculiar Simla is eccentric in its fashion of treating friendships" (89) Pankaj K Singh's words may be appropriate to sum up this tendency,

While for hegemonic structures, be they of caste, class, gender, race or antion, literary representation has been a potential instrument of manipulating, silencing, or mis-representing the oppressed, for the dispossessd victims literary representation is the only empowering site to register their protest and contest oppressive hegemonies. The poetics of the literature of the marginalised or the subalterns of the oppressed can never be a matter of pure aesthetics, political stance is an integral part of their literary creativity (18-20).

The tribal population of India, whose representation (in literature) is the representation subject of this study, account for more than eight percent of the Indian population These are the people who many claim are the indigenous inhabitants of the peninsula which later came to be known as Bharata or Aryavarta after the new race of Aryans who invaded the militarily less advanced people of the Indian peninsula and subjugated them to a secondary position in the society It is asserted by Sarat Chandra Roy in The Mundas and Their Country (1912) that these are the peoples whose remote ancestors were once masters of Indian soil, whose joys and sorrows, once made up the history of the Indian peninsula (Dasgupta 136), and who upon successive invasions of the Indian peninsula and even after the domination of the earlier conquerors by the later conquerors (which continued as one wave after the other over many centuries and millennia), remained perpetually in domination ever since they lost the first of the most decisive battles' for their respected place in their own society. To their dismay since the first of such battles, much before the birth of Christ, the rise of Buddhism or Islam, they were never really going to regain the lost ground. Those who prized themselves and their standing among others and those who feared for the well-being of their fellow brethren fled deep into the forests across all parts of the country and very rarely came into contact with those who were responsible for their plight.

This would, however, be an oversimplification of history. The Aryan invasion theory is marred in controversy as there is no certainty about the authenticity of the Aryan settler/original inhabitants story, and the politics of the state hangs on its truth claim" (Spivak 327). What is true nonetheless is that in the darkness of the forest they limited their activities to satisfying the most basic and essential needs for mere survival. They hunted animals and gathered other items of food, shelter and protection. They lived on subsistence level and in the process, over different parts of such settlements, developed their own cultures and dogmas and taboos. They lived in closely knit clans, mostly under a headman or a chief They formed their own customs and rules, many of which were determined and governed by the circumstances and conditions that surrounded them. In the midst of all these 'hostile conditions and societies there is only one thing they succeeded in protecting and which is something they cherished the most - Freedom.

Outside these forest settlements, the mainstream society continued to look at the forest societies with curiosity, animosity, suspicion, occasional patronisation and sometimes even compassion and understanding With the passage of time, they continued to be known by various denominators The terms that were thrown up from time to time were different and varying even though the subjects of such nomenclature remained what they were bound to be, irrespective of the terms that they were identified by, by the world outside their own which was less inclined to help them in any way than keeping themselves busy by devising new methods of keeping them in their place of subjugation and domination.

In the two great Indian epics, the Ramayana and the Mahabharata, reference is made to such individuals belonging to these forest communities, Shabrı, Kewat, Shambuk (Ramayana) and Aeklauya (Mahabharata) These individuals and their societies are shown to hold the mainstream society, especially the royalty with utmost devotion and respect. However, their alienation and the apparent social stratifaction is manifest in the polemic guru dakshina episode of Dronacharya from Aiklavya in the Mahabharata. The relationship between the forest-dwellers (vanavasi) and the rulers has verily attained a poitical dimension here. Nevertheless the dividing line between the rural and the vanavasi in the traditional Indian society was very thin for the simple fact that the villages largely depended on the forests for their sustenance Rabindranath Tagore has described the Indian civilisation as Aranyak Sanstriti. The gurukuls were located in the forests. Kalidas's Abhijnan Shakuntalam best describes the nature of relationship between the forest dwellers and the ruling class, on the one hand and among the animate and inanimate objects on the other.

Given the sensitivity of the task at hand the agency of representation should ideally be 'instructed' to show a genuine understanding of the subject and thus if not show favour to the represented then at least-avoid maligning it. As has been pointed out, a great amount of effort and caution is required to dislodge dominant modes of representation and challenge the hegemonic force of representation"(Dimri 64).

Ever since the dawn of civilisation and its gradual evolution, literature has played a crucial role in the society, primarily for two reasons One, it lends legitimacy or at least some sort of sanction to the subject. Secondly, in earlier times, due to lack of other media, the written manuscripts and other books, particularly the ones with a religious backing, had tremendous influence on the people's psyche and their collective consciousness.

In a caste ridden society like in India, the written literature had far reaching consequences on the social set up. It is as a result of such impact of literature on the masses that Wendy Doniger (2009) rightly claims that the Dharm Shastra of Manu is the one text that is mostly set on fire by the dalit protestors.

The result of such misrepresentation "legitimises", to an extent, the methods of such oppression. Considering the position of the tribals in the ancient Indian society, one can sec that they were not a part of the varna system, despite the fact that it was in itself discriminatory. This sometimes led to the belief that they were not fit enough to be humans beings as such. Though Tulsidasa's Ramacharitmanas is a much later text, it reflects the attitude of the mainstream society towards the tribal population of not just the age when it was written but also of the age that it describes. The entire epic is strewn with the examples of the vanavasis being of the subhuman category. The tribal characters are themselves depicted as conceding their "barbarity" to the royals of Ayodhaya. Upon meeting the exiled Rama, the Kols, Kiratas, Bhils and the other forest dwellers say, "Indeed our greatest service is not to steal and run off with your utensils and clothes! Unfeeling creatures are we, often taking others' lives, crooked by nature, wicked, evil-minded and base-born" (II 250).

The tribal characters in the epic are in a way made to accept their baseness and it becomes a common reference point for the posterity What is however, problematically and conveniently forgotten or ignored, is the mention in the text, that the forest dwellers offer a variety of products to the exiled party without accepting any price for it and even showing unhappiness if they insisted in paying anything. This nobility on the part of the forest dwellers seems to be conveniently ignored by commentators and just in case some might notice such occasions and even glorify the forest community for such show of hospitality, the text is quick to add:

> *You are all virtuous and we are vile Nishadas, it is only by the grace of Rama that we have been blessed with the sight of you show us your grace, and in order to gratify us, accept our fruit and herbs and shoots. You have come to this forest as our welcome guests, but we are not fortunate enough to be worthy of doing any service to you What can we offer you, noble sirs? Fuel and leaves are the only tokens of a Kirata's friendship! (II, 249-50).*

In a significant way the text is unfair to the forest dwellers. The people who are capable of such noble virtues as hospitability and peaceful meeting, are presented to be such only because they seem to be overwhelmed by the gorge of separation between the 'virtue of the noble race of Ayodhaya and vicious nature of the vile forest dwellers and repeatedly such show of character by the forest dwellers is described as a result of the grace of lord Rama.

Add to such description the viewpoint of the various religious texts and the holy scriptures on the issues of caste and tribes in ancient India. Drawing from Romila Thapar and G. S. Ghurye, Wendy Doniger writes,

> *Many of the assimilated castes were Shudras, who were excluded from participating in the Vedic rituals Below the Shudras were the so-called polluted castes, beside, rather below them, were the tribals and unassimilated aliens (mlecchas). The logic of class placed some tribal groups in a castelike category, albeit one standing outside the caste hierarchy, tribals are relegated not to a distinct level within a vertical structure, but rather to a horizontal annex that could not be integrated into any cubbyhole in the system (285).*

What such a biased attitude of the scriptures, coupled by the resultant arrogance of the society does to that particular group in the society is what Doniger terms as a cold-blooded disregard in real life. Describing the incident of the treacherous burning alive of a Nishad woman and her five sons in the fateful house of lac, where the Pandavas and Kunti escaped unhurt, Doniger points out the alarming silence of the text as, 'Only the single word "innocent" (without wrongdoing) suggests the slightest syrapathy for the murdered Nishadas They arc sacrificial substitutes, whom the author of this text treats as expendable because he regards them as subhuman beings. Perhaps their drunkenness (one of the four addictive vices of lust) is meant to justify their deaths (288).

In a similar tone, the incident of the guru-dakshina sought by Drona and inimediately complied by the Nishada prince Ekalavya is mentioned in the epic as a matter of fact incident. Doniger asks:

...where is the author's sympathy? It is hard to be sure. It is arrogant of Ekalavya to push in where he does not belong, he cannot be a noble archer, for he was born into the wrong family for nobility But Ekalavya does not act arrogant. His outward appearance invokes all the conventional tropes for tribals he is described as black, wrapped in black deerskin, hair all matted, dressed in rags, his body caked with dirt He is made of the wrong stuff (or as we would say, has the wrong genes). He is physically dirty But his inner soul, reflected in his behavior, is pious and respectful, he does what the teacher tells him to do, not only is he a brilliant archer, but he is honest and humble (289).

Such representation of the forest dwellers (now mostly clubbed as tribals) in the popular literatures and then in relegation to an inferior status in society create a formidable situation for not just the tribals but even other such wronged classes in the society, where their exploitation and domination goes almost unnoticed and is sometimes, even justified since they are widely believed to be 'vile, vicious, criminal and conveniently dispensable. Ever since the epic ages onwards the tribal community has continued to be harassed and misunderstood in some way or the other. But with the arrival of the British empire, the situation deteriorated many folds. The new colonial masters wanted to know so that its utilization could be maximised.

In the pre-colonial period, the Indian society had consisted of Hindus and non- Hindus. Among the non-Hindus, there were numerous sections, living aloof from each other and from the mainstream society at the same time. Some of these sections were at various degrees of Hinduisation and Sanskritisation but were characterised chiefly by the absence of caste system or the jati hierarchy Till the advent and further consolidation of the British empire, a marked contrast between these sections of forest dwellers (who later came to be known as 'tribes) and the common society of the mainstream India was absent. They were not two fundamentally different sections in the collective consciousness of India or in the psyche of the common India, leave alone the constitutional or state recognition of it. They were a part of a society that had numerous sections with various occupations and each at a different level of socio- economic development. Niharranjan Ray writes:

In the literary sources The communities of people whom today we refer to as 'tribe' and those that we know from history as belonging to more advanced stages of socio-economic and cultural growth, there is hardly any evidence to show that in the collective mind of India, communities of people there was any consciousness of a difference between the two sets of janas except in the matter of jati, that is, in the matter of socio-religious and economic organization alone. These janas whom we have been taught to call tribes', were indeed different from the other communities of people only in the sense that they continued to remain outside the control of the jati system of social organisation (9).

The British empire building machine, in order to set up an administrative mechanism, generalized and oversimplified the social realities of India. The empire introduced the study of anthropology to know its people in order to 'administer" them more appropriately. L.KA. lyer, one of the leading anthropologists in pre-independent India noted in 1925, "The work hitherto done in Indian Anthropology has been mainly for administrative purpose. But nothing worthy of the name has been done to ascertain the types persisting in a country to which no other country in the world can be compared as possessing so many varieties" (Kalpana Ram 73).

It was, however, not in the use of this science as such that the seeds of domination were sown but in the application of that 'knowledge' which Claude Levi-Strauss noted in 1965, "Anthropology is daughter to [an] era of violence whereby the larger part of humanity had been rendered subservient to the minority and millions of people thrown into bondage" (Deshpande et al 2007. 12). The forest dwellers were identified as 'the tribes The clutches of the empire had to penetrate into the length, breath, width and depth of the country that to many westerners is still enigmatic and that J.K. Galbraith was astonished enough to call a functional anarchy, even many years after independence.

The impression of the adivasis in the popular psyche as brutes, murderers and uncivilized made it easy for the imperial government to manoeuvre them, almost always ruthlessly. The Criminal Tribes Act of 1871 declared men and women belonging to many tribes 'criminal by birth It was a point in the history of imperial India where it became abundantly clear what happens to a people who have throughout been on the wrong side of history, sociology and even geography, not just in material reality but even in the psyche of the civilisation. The entire social groups were declared criminal by birth, hunted, captured and imprisoned by the police, made to work as bonded labour in public works and their sexual activities prevented by a strict surveillance. In the protection of the Act, their lands became publically available to predators and their forest resources became available to be exploited by the empire ever in need for more such resources and their unrestricted exploitation.

Gopinath Mohanty's *Paraja* is a seminal text in portraying how easy it is to trap the tribals into exploitation and also, how shockingly convenient it is for the oppressor to get away with the deed despite the presence of the police and judiciary The government officials, hand in glove with the local landlords, subject the poor and often unsuspecting tribals to misery. The ordeal for the otherwise happy and a prosperous family begins when Sukru Jani stands up to protect the honour of his daughters Jili and Bili. The government official, in this case the forest guard, finds it extremely simple to ask for one of the daughters to gratify his lust, knowing well the hapless tribal family will have no one to protect them once he shows them his disfavour.

Similarly, the struggle for the rights to the forest resources in Mahashweta Devi's *Aranyer Adhikar* is scoffed at by the imperial government who needed the timber for not just the railways but also to build their ships. In the process of acquiring the vast wealth of the forests, the government did not hesitate to destroy a complete way of life, culture and civilisation By constantly portraying them as uncivilised and backward, the government found it easier to justify its acts of greed and violence.

Stephen Corry shows us how the tribal people are portrayed not just in Indian media but worldwide. He writes in an article Loot of Tribal Resources Masquerades As Progress in The Times of India (2006):

Terms like primitive' imply that tribal people are inferior to the rest of us. Apologists for the so-called progress or the kind of development mentioned above may tell you otherwise, but there really is no way of measuring human worth that enables us to say one culture is any better than another. Of course, you can measure things like life expectancy and level of illness, but the terrific irony of this is that forced settlement of tribal peoples invariably results in shorter lives and more disease Ultimately, tribal people live differently from us and do and

Such contaminated' expressions about the tribal societies lead not just to ignorance about the reality of their situation but even hatred for them, since it is only a minority of the mainstream society who have any interaction with the real tribal society and the majority rely only on the information that has been passed on to them by others. Sarat Chandra Roy noted in 1938: "Any one will be struck by the amount of injustice done, in spite of the best intentions, by judges and magistrates and police officers of all grades, owing to their ignorance of the customs and mentality of the aboriginal tribes they have to deal with" (Dasgupta 143).

The result of universal misunderstanding or prejudice against those we don't really understand or even attempt to understand often results in colossal damage to the misunderstood or the misrepresented. We may be reminded of the earlier arguments of Ranajit Guha how careless and prejudiced 'comment' slowly 'worms its way' into a 'fact' and, thereafter, such facts could be stretched to any extent so long as it can be justified in terms of public conscience. Even in the modern Indian nation state this stereotypical image is exploited by the democratic government to justify the persecution of the tribal people.

This point is reiterated as Corry brings out into the public consciousness the facts that the governments claim that forcibly developing tribal peoples is for their own good and helps them to catch up with so-called civilization, when often all they really want is to exploit the vast natural wealth of many tribal people's land The result of this development is almost always catastrophic poverty, alcoholism, prostitution, disease and early death" (2006). The Booker Prize winning activist author Arundhati Roy mentions in The Shape of the Beast that "... it is estimated that up to 56 million people could have been displaced in this country in the last fifty years sparking a question as to what percentage of the people who plan these mammoth projects are dalit, adivasi or even rural?"(2008).

It is, therefore, of great importance that genuine representation be made of those who are often vulnerable not just to be sidelined and exploited but also to being represented by others. The above discussion highlights the dreadful repercussions of such mindless representation of the subjugated classes. Portrayal of a group of people or culture through various channels such as literature, historical writing, socio- political commentaries and in the modern print and electronic media including films are the necessary ingredients which form the basis of our social consciousness and shape our understanding of not just our own society but various others sections that constitute the entire fabric of our national and internation society.

The vast tribal population of India, which is more than eight percent of the total Indian population, still sits on the outskirts of the psyche of the mainstream India, waiting to be understood and acknowledged as fellow citizens. The gap between the two, that has existed over the millennia, is yet to be bridged as "...the mainstream 'Indian culture is as distant from the aboriginal subaltern in India as is Aristotle"(Spivak 333). Even their contribution to the course of our socio-economic and political history is undermined since "We have yet a very primitive understanding of the social composition, culture and ideology of many of the tribal and peasant movements in twentieth century India" (Ramchandra Guha 6).

Until the very recent past, and even after independence, the tribal population has always stood on the margins of Indian political and cultural scene. The distance maintained on both the sides has sometimes magnified between the 'original' and 'alien' inhabitants of the land. The focus brings in the perennially alive discussion of who came from where' or even 'who came first' and an answer was attempted when the Aryan Invasion theory was formulated. Shashi Tharoor observes:

If the phrase "ethnic melting pot' had been coined two thousand years ago, India would have had a fair claim to the title. The "Indigenous people", around 1500 B.C., were probably dark-skinned Dravidians, with aboriginals of Negroid stock in many forests. Then came the great wave of Aryan migration from the Central Asian steppes. The Aryans were pale skinned and light eyed nomads whose search for new homeland branched into three waves, one stopping in Persia, one sweep continuing on to Europe as far as Germany, and the other descending into India....This common heritage explains why the Nazis in Germany used a variation of the Swastika, an Aryan religious symbol still revered by Indian Hindus (11).

It is then this torrent of the Aryan invasion which dominated or even destroyed the then prevailing indigenous culture in the northern part of India. Since the "intruders brought with them a more superior civilisation" in terms of military skills, the written language (as Max Muller calls the Aryans of India the framers of the most wonderful language Sanskrit) and the power of organisation, the indigenous population either perished or joined the Aryans as dasa meaning slaves. The ones who wanted to retain their way of living hid into the forests and continued to dwell there, many of whom can still be said to be there.

As the Aryan invasion theory suggests, they gradually spread all over the northern part of India and chose not to trouble the forest dwellers except when they needed the forest resources such as timber, elephants and any such thing. The forest dwellers on their part remained a threat to these Aryan settlements and never shied away from invading and looting these for food and cattle and then retreating into the darkness and the wildness of the forests. These could indeed be retaliatory proceedings but not much can actually be said about these except that the two communities showed suspicion and hostility towards each other. Aryans being superior controled the major and the more fertile part of the sub-continent.

The Aryan invasion theory has drawn flak from many quarters. Romila Thapar, an eminent historian, notes how the theory has been vulnerable to political games over the last century. She gives two examples on the extreme ends of this confrontation. One is, "Jyotiba Phule, an authority on the Dalits, who argued in the late nineteenth century that the Sanskrit-speaking Brahmans were descended from the Aryans who were alien to India, and that the indigenous peoples of the lower castes were therefore the rightful inheritors of the land. This argument assumes a conflict between the dominant upper caste and the conquered, oppressed lower castes. This was the foundation of caste confrontation and an explanation for caste hierarchy" (14).

This was the caste based outcome of the reaction to the theory. The other reactions come from the other extreme that Thapar writes of as based on Hindu nationalism and what has come to be called as the Hindutva ideology. Since the early twentieth century, this view has gradually shifted from supporting the theory of an invasion to denying such an event, now arguing that the Aryans and their language, Sanskrit, were indigenous to India. The importance of this confrontation with the Aryan Invasion theory lies in its shift of focus from caste to religion as Thapar points out,

> *The focus moved from caste to religion the aliens were not the upper castes, but Muslims and Christians whose religion was organized in west Asia. The communists were also added to this group for good measure! According to this theory only the Hindus, as the lineal descendants of the Aryans, could be defined as indigenous and therefore the*

inheritors of the land, and not even those whose ancestry was of the subcontinent, but who had been converted to Islam and Christianity (14).

Such kind of contestation of the Aryan invasion theory finds other supporters too apart from the Hindu Nationalists, in David Frowley and Navaratna S. Rajaram who call it 'politics of history' and the 'subversion of scholarship' as many believe the theory was propagated by the British to create divisions in the Indian society and also to legitimise British rule over India since the theory rendered them as not the only 'aliens' dominating the 'natives. Since the Aryan invasion theory is outside the purview of this study, a brief mention of it must be sufficient to understand the past and locate the tribal population amidst all this turmoil.

The entire Indian subcontinent can be divided into three geographical divisions namely, the mountain chain in the north from west to east, the largest mountain range in the world, the Himalayas, secondly, the great Indo-Gangetic plain and thirdly, the Peninsula.

The mountain chain in the north, writes A.L. Basham, divides India from the rest of Asia and the world. The barrier, however, was at one time an inseparable one, and at all periods both settlers and traders have found their way over the high and desolate passes into India, while Indians have carried their commerce and cultures beyond her frontiers by the same route. India's isolation has never been complete.

Ironically the mighty chain of the north provided no such immunity' to the indigenous people of the land.

Various races came in the course of history, dominated the natives and though they may have assimilated certain cultural traits of the latter, by and large, these invaders converted them to their own order or pushed them into oblivion, forests and other inaccessible areas.

From time to time, with the advancement of navigation, the coasts too proved to be paths of intrusion though not all such intrusions may have had ill effects on the natives. It may never be easy to identify how the 'original' natives were but the ones who once settled, became, in their own way, natives for yet new comers with whatever motive they came. Shashi Tharoor writes:

Over the centuries, India witnessed the mingling of Greeks, Scythians, and Parthians; Mongols, Huns and Chinese; and as assortment of mercenary warriors from central Asia, Iran, Turkey, and even Ethiopia. As they inter-married with each other and with the local population, the Indian melting pot produced a people with a variety of skin colors and every physiognomic features imaginable, as a look at any Indian cricket, hockey, or soccer team will confirm (1).

These teams mentioned above may still not confirm it as much as the parliament of India which leave not much to represent the diverse people of a huge country that Churchill thought of as a mere geographical expression' and 'no more a single country than the Equator' (Tharoor 1) and the modern administration, which J.K. Galbraith, former US ambassador to India, called a 'functional anarchy.

All along this 'barrier' of the north we have, surviving to the present day, pockets of tribal population, some with very distinct identity, from the remote areas of Afghanistan to the north-east of India. Encyclopedia Asiatica describes these tribes as follows: "Dr. W.W. Hunter has mentioned that in the North-West provinces there are wandering and wild tribes named Bur, Damak..."(53) Then follows a long list of these tribes all over India including the ones in Nepal and Ceylon. The northeast, as Tharoor mentions, "... embraces a wide diversity of cultural stains, from the tribal traditions of the Nagas and the Mizos to the mainstream Hinduism of Manipur.....The people range from Bengali Migrants in Tripura and Assam to the Christian hill folk of Nagaland, whose official state language is English, to anglicized tea planters and aborigines with bones through their noses" (12).

The Indo- Gangetic Plain, due to its rivers and their tributaries and vast fertile lands were an open invitation to settlers and invaders alike. "These are also optimal areas", as Romila Thapar writes in Early India, "for the rise of urban centres (43). According to Tharoor, immigrants, invaders, and visitors, whether their intentions were warlike or peaceful usually made for the Gangetic plain, the fertile stretch of land that gave birth to the Indo-Aryan civilization over three thousand years ago (11). In terms of centres of civilisation that came into existence, Indus valley had earliest ones, followed by the Ganges, a larger of the western part of the Ganges plain has been that focus point or the region for the civilisation of the Aryans. Since the Gangetic plains were thickly forested in certain areas the possibility of small pockets of 'tribal societies' existing amidst the centres of Aryan civilisation can not be ruled out.

The Peninsula is the southern part of the country with Arabian sea on the Western and Bay of Bangai on the eastern side. According to Romila Thapar, "Urbanization in the peninsula dates to the late Mauryan period and the start of the first millennium A.D. but there is considerable and impressive pre-urban activity in many areas" (45).

This pre-urban activity suggests that the so called tribal societies existed there since a much earlier period. According to Thapar,

> *The mountains and plateaus of central India, with their dense forests, tended to get bypassed by migrants and settlers for many centuries. The major settlements were along the more frequented routes from the northern plains southwards to the Deccan. These settlements made only a marginal impact on the forest dwellers until later centuries when encroachments into the forests for timber and elephants, as well as cultivable land became more common. Central India was regarded as the major habitat of 'tribal societies' and forest peoples, even though such societies were scattered throughout the subcontinent, pockets of which continue to the present (45).*

How these societies differed from the neighboring peasant societies could be seen in the centrality of plough agriculture and tenancies (in terms of land, livelihood). However, in recent time these elements have also entered the lifestyle of the tribal societies. Thapar further writes, "Far to the east are the Andaman and Nicobar Islands, closer to south east Asia than India perhaps the people living there were not so welcoming. In the last couple of centuries the people of the islands have been studied by colonial anthropologists, attempting to define the 'primitive' " (47)

In recent times a lot of interest has been generated in the academic circles and civil society about the other India, Aryans or non- Aryans, who have, throughout history, been pushed on to the margins and forced to survive amidst hostility, hatred, indifference and poverty. It is nothing short of miracle that many such societies still exist in India without having lost their survival methods, though they may have rearranged themselves from time to time according to their surroundings. These surroundings range from climate changes to encroachment on their lands to sheer power and presence of superior organised society around them and efforts of this society to civilise them.

It would be naïve to imagine that the indigenous people simply vanished from the scene once the onslaught of the Aryan civilisation began somewhere in the second millennium B.C. They had enormous impact on the way civilisation and culture took shape in the sub-continent. It is true that the Aryan urban system was more complex in organisation than the indigenous ones, as Romila Thapar mentions and these complex societies were obviously more dominant and elbowed their way into history. Others were forced to be more reticent but they did not disappear. It is often in the interface of such differing societies that the patterns of Indian culture were foraged. As the living prehistory of India, their survival albeit even in forms that have changed somewhat over time and their presence in history has to be recognized" (56).

Romila Thapar suggests that at that earlier stage the indigenous people and/or the marginal ones can be categorised into two groups; the hunter gatherers and the pastoralists. The Aryans or the dominant groups can be studied as peasants and townsmen. The hunter gatherers were the least organised of the lot. They were at the lowest level of subsistence and merely survived. Their survival depended on hunting animals in forest area and gathering other food items chiefly from the forests. These groups or bands of people did not have much to do with the other parts of the society, i.e., the ones who lived in areas outside the society. They had no clearly demarcated areas except that they probably thought of the forested areas as their natural habitats and had not many occasions of interaction with the outsiders.

The special characteristic of these people was that they were devoid of any social status or social hierarchy. There were no inferiors or superiors in the group. They lived in bands or family or at the most as a group of people of a few families joined together by kinship. This group developed into a clan. At that early stage these people did not practice agriculture and keep animals for any practical use except hunting the wild ones for food.

The role of the forest to these people could be well understood as a forest to them was more than just an environment for food. It was 'home' for them, it sheltered them from the outsiders, it provided them with caves and resources of various types for food.

Thapar adds further that the demarcation between what was called the grama, village, and the aranya, forest or wildness, and later the kshetra, literally field, and the vana, forest, reflects a perceived opposition between the two systems. In actual practice the dichotomy was not so sharp and the one faded into the other, but the divide was maintained in theory. The forest was the unknown, the wild, the unpredictable whereas the settlement was predictable and subject to known laws. Fantasies about the people of the forest, be they apsaras, celestial maidens, or rakshashas, demons, occur more frequently in the earlier literature.

It was, therefore, when the outside world encroached upon the forests for resources, that the forest dwellers retaliated, often destroying their crops and stealing their cattle. Tulsidas in Ramacharitamanas, in trying to recreate the glory of those earlier times, on numerous occasions depicts the forests and the forest dwellers as abominable and intolerable. Nishadaraj tells Lord Rama that his people and he himself can do nothing better than steal other people's things and run away with them. The scriptures thus painted a picture of these forest dwellers as asuras, demons, as opposed to surs, the deities. The physical gap and absence of interaction between them probably allowed the misconception to not just exist but even develop further into more misunderstanding and prejudice.

With the passage of time and with somewhat confrontational and other interactions with peasants, forest dwellers began certain other practices that were hitherto absent from their normal existence. Thapar refers to Banabhatta, writing in the seventh century A.D, as he described them in his Harshacharita, that some of those groups in certain areas had, been acculturated and their activities and occupations had become somewhat similar to those of the neighboring peasants. She adds:

Forest dwellers were not confined to being hunter-gatherers. Some were shifting cultivators, or were horticulturalists, and some practiced sedentary cultivation. Their societies were organized in clans and the larger unit was the tribe; this organization distinguished them from peasant cultivators and caste society. Social hierarchy received little attention and generally the differentiation was only between the chief, who had the highest status, and the other clansmen. Status and bonding based on kinship relations were more common. They had a preference for living in forests and used a limited technology, their religion was largely animistic, their rituals and beliefs created by shamuns, and their isolation permitted them to use their own language (56).

A.L. Basham mentions how at one time practically the whole of India was inhabited by such peoples, and in ancient and medieval times they were more in numbers than the villagers and occupied a wider area than at present. He goes on to add how the tribesmen continued to exist in the outlying districts on virtual independence, perhaps occasionally paying tribute in kind to the representative of their overlord. At all times the wild tribesmen were a danger to the settled villagers in the outlying parts of the country. In medieval literature, both in Sanskrit and the Dravidian vernaculars, there are references to these wild raiders pillaging crops and herds and houses, and capturing victims for human sacrifice. The area of their operations was gradually pushed back, and as more and more primitive tribes were submitted to the Hindu order they became gradually less dangerous; but throughout.... They were a source of fear in many parts of India... (197-8).

The second category was that of the pastoralists who were nomadic people, practicing little agriculture at times. They were carriers of goods' with rearing of cattle as their another major occupation. Some of them migrated large distances in order to do business with inhabitants of various areas. These bands or clans explored new pastures for their cattle and also used forest areas, especially in summer seasons when there is not much snow there. Among them the Banjuras, Gaddi and Gujjars, to name just a few, are still active and continue their type and method of occupation based on migration and temporary settlement. They could be categorised as:

    i. Four types of societies: Hunter-Gatherers/ Pastoralists/Peasants/Townsmen.

ii. Castes and the Tribal Standing vis-a-vis castes. (Thapar 58)

Since these people needed to exist together for reasons of livelihood, business and security, therefore, it was natural for them to form clans based on kinship. This was an effective way of migrating successfully, warding of dangers and also to seize property and goods from others. Among pastoralists, membership of a tribe generally included those claiming common grazing ground and descent from a common ancestor, with a common language and custom, as well as rituals. The creation of a tribe could be occasioned by political needs when searching for new pastures or attacking sedentary societies. Thapar clearly mentions, "The tribe can be viewed as seminary, moving away from the family as the nucleus to larger entities such as lineages which were identified by a common, mythical ancestor. Where descent was unilateral the emphasis was on kinship, whether actual or fictive" (59).

Thapar describes two types of pastoralists. On the one hand were those who arrived in India from central Asia such as Parhians, Shakas, Kushanas, Hunas and Turks. The other group is more domestic, the 'cattle-keepers of the peninsula. As a component of agriculture and exchange, these filled in the spaces between peasant societies. Cattle keepers, apart from providing dairy produce, also acted as carriers of commodities for exchange.

How these pastoralists in particular differed from the hunter gatherers is that the pastoralists had a good deal of interaction with the peasantry. They were into trade and other exchanges with the peasant class and therefore are not so demonised in the common psyche, though, they too might have been on the receiving end in terms of power, culture and social standing.

Next in the social ladder came the peasants. They were different from the other two mentioned classes as these people were well settled on their land holdings, they tilled their soil and cultivated their land from one generation to another. They were identified by the village or the areas they lived in. The peasant class was very important from the social as well as the standpoint of the state as these were the revenue providers for their rulers. The government of the day had direct power over them and their resources of all kinds and in return they were promised security from external posers.

A prominent feature of the peasantry was the presence of a strict, social hierarchy which, as has been discussed, was totally absent in the society of hunter-gatherers and the pastoralists, and as compared to clans based on kin-relations, the peasantry was marked by castes.

The next society was that of the people who inhabited the towns. The towns were centres for the capital city and other concentrations for military and state machinery. This is where the writ of the government of the day ran supreme as these towns were efficiently managed by the system of the state. Romila Thapar writes that there was a more marked division in the specialised characteristic of towns as compared to villages. The authors also mentions that the heterogeneity of urban life distinguished it from the village. Towns were closely packed settlements with populations larger than those in a village. Norms of social behavior tended to be more flexible, and heterodox ideas were often developed in urban centres or in places associated with these. Early brahmanical normative texts tend to disapprove of the town, although in later works this view changes.

The state had an attitude of domination, patronisation and exploitation towards the tribes settled in the forests. The tribal concentration was always a threat to the settled populations who paid revenue to the state. A.L. Basham gives an account of the state of the tribals in relation to the administration of Asoka,

> *...Asoka was not a complete pacifist. The wild tribesmen of hill and forest were a constant source of danger to the more settled parts of the empire, and it would seem that earlier kings had kept them in check by ruthless campaign of extermination. Asoka clearly intend to try to civilize them, but is quite evident that he was ready to repress them by force if they continued their raids on the more settled parts of his empire. In Asoka's own word: the beloved of the Gods even reasons with the forest tribes in his empire, and seeks to reform them' (54).*

But Asoka does not end here. In case of non-compliance the emperor had his solution cut out for the uncivilised tribesmen. He continues, "But the beloved of the Gods is not only compassionate, he is also powerful and he tells them to repent, less they be slain" (54)

Caste and Tribal Society

Tribal society, despite its different behavioral pattern and life style that leads many to condemn it as uncivilised and savage, deserves appreciation for being without hierarchy, especially castes, which plagues the mainstream society that prides in calling itself civilised. The only hierarchy that existed initially, and still exists in many tribal societies is that between the chief of the tribe and the rest of the people. In addition to the headman, who generally 'won' his position through valour and strength and not on the law of inheritance, the chief priest enjoyed a somewhat superior position since it was he who played the intermediary role between the god and his people. This is, however, not to suggest that the tribal societies remained untouched by the caste system forever.

The following pages demonstrate how castes came into existence and secondly, how some tribal societies acquired some of the characteristics of the system or even remained virtually immune from it. The terms that have to be scanned here are varna, Jana and Jati. The early Vedic corpus divided the society into four varnas-brahmans (priest), kshatriya (warrior), vaishya (cultivators or trader) and on the lowest step stood the shudra (whose duty was to serve the other three varnas). This system divided the society into four basic groups and it was indeed an oppressive system to keep the society in permanently drawn compartments. The various functions were clearly laid out and adherence to the four varnas was strictly followed.

With the Aryans beginning to dominate the aboriginals of northern part of the sub-continent, it became a matter of pride and necessity for the fair-skinned minority to maintain superiority over the dark-skinned majority. 'Purity' was at the centre of the Varna system, and therefore, the dark majority of the aboriginals were accorded a place at the very lowest in the Aryan hierarchy.

Caste system came into play at later stages. The number of varna remained the same and various castes were born out of the existing social structure which became more complex with time. The word used for caste is jati which is derived from a root meaning 'birth' (Thapar 63). It is a possibility that various castes developed in the social system and their place in the society was determined by the varna that they had been allotted. The origin of 'caste' is difficult to ascertain but some people from the same lineage, practicing the same profession or occupation or means of livelihood probably formed a 'caste and had a relative place in hierarchy corresponding to their varna, therefore, derermining the difference between the so called 'high' and 'low' castes.

According to Romila Thapar, for a society to become a caste based society there have to be three preconditions; the society must register social disparities, there has to be unequal access of various groups within that society to economic resources, and inequalities should be legitimised through theoretically irreversible hierarchy and the imposition of the hierarchy claims to be based on a super-natural authority (64).

Jati and *varna* system co-existed and whereas varna didn't increase in number, jatis grew unaccountably, and so complex has the Indian social system grown over the years that it is almost impossible to either note all the social categories in terms of castes and groups or to see their mutual relationship. Jatis have never really sought sanction from varna system but each of them inevitably belongs to one varna or the other. Each varna, for example Brahmans, are also divided into several - sub-castes, some 'purer' than the other and, therefore, 'superior. In this context A.L.Basham's remarks are worth mentioning:

> *When the Portuguese came to India in the 16th century they found the Hindu community divided into many separate groups, which they called castas meaning tribes, clans or families. The name stuck, and became the usual word for the Hindu social group.......castes rise and fall in the social scale, and old castes die out and new ones are formed, but the four great classes are stable........The two systems have never been thoroughly harmonized (148).*

However, the mutual existence and sometimes, even the over-lapping of the varna and the jati systems have never really created much confusion among people as they very well understand their relative positions. John Keay notes, "If Varna provided the theoretical framework, jati came to represent the practical reality" (53).

In this context Dr. Radhakrishan's comments are noteworthy:

When the Aryans came to India through the Punjab they found the natives of India whom they called dasyus opposing their free advance. These dasyus were of a dark complexion, eating beef and indulging in goblin worship. When the Aryans met them they desired to keep themselves aloof from them. It is this spirit of exclusiveness born of pride of race and superiority of culture that developed into the later caste spirit... Originally occupational, the division soon became hereditary..... The system of caste is in reality neither Aryan nor Dravidian, but was introduced to meet the needs of the time when the different racial types had to live together in amity (75).

It is not that the system had no drawbacks. Radhakrishnan notes three major shortcomings. Firstly, what prevented social organisation from decay and death ultimately prevented it from growing. Secondly, the barriers didn't weaken when the tide of progress demanded it. And thirdly, the preserved social order didn't help the advancement of the nation as a whole (75).

Radhakrishnan, however, does not miss the point that this intermingling had some contributions too. He notes that only caste made it possible for a number of races to live together side by side without fighting each other. Also, India solved peacefully the inter-racial problem which other people did by a decree of death. In addition, caste enabled the Vedic Indians to preserve the integrity and independence of the conquering as well as the conquered races and promote mutual confidence and harmony unlike the European races, which, upon conquering others, took care to efface their human dignity and annihilate their self respect (75),

Varna and *jati* thus became the inseparable parts of the mainstream society where jana, i.e., the clan (which later came to be designated as the tribe in the colonial times) was a separated entity in the early times. John Keay observes:

> *Beyond the pale of the Arya were a variety of indigenous peoples like the despised dasa of Vedas, All were, nevertheless, subject to varying degrees of Aryanisation. In Buddhist texts, and in common parlance even today, the more usual word for caste is not varna but jati. Jati derives from a verb meaning 'to be born', the emphasis being less on the degree of ritual purity, as in the four-tier varna, and more on caste determination as a result of being born into a particular kinship group. If varna provided the theoretical framework jati came to represent the practical reality...geographical, tribal, sectarian and, above all, economic and professional specialisations determined a group's jati (54).*

In the words of Dr.S. Radhakrishan, "The Vedic Aryans, as they advanced into India came across uncivilized tribes, wild and barbarous, and worshipping snakes and serpents, stocks and stones. No society can hope to continue in a state of progressive civilisation in the midst of uncivilized and half-civilised tribes, if it does not meet and overcome the new situation by either completely conquering them or imparting to them elements of its own culture" (118).

Presumably, the only option open before the Aryans was to mix with the natives and in a way 'absorb' them to their system and to attempt to "raise them to a higher level". Radhakrishnan adds further that, "While the Rig-Veda describes the period of conflict between the fair-skinned Aryans and the dark dasyus, which Indian mythology makes into a strife of devas and rakshasas, the Atharva Veda speaks of the period when the conflict is settled and the two are trying to live in harmony by mutual give and take" (119). It was thus natural that in this give and take both sides should lose some of its original characteristics and assimilate a few of the others. It was during those centuries of inter mingling that a society of somewhat mixed characteristics was shaped as Radhakrishnan elaborates, "The worship of spirits and stars, trees and mountains and other superstitions of jungle tribes crept into the Vedic religion. The effort of the Vedic Aryan to educate the uncivilised resulted in the corruption of the ideal which he tried to spread... such are the revenges which the weak of the world have on the strong... when the Aryan and the non-Aryan religions, one refined and the other vulgar, the one good and the other base, met, there was the tendency for the bad to beat the good out of circulation" (119).

In a similar tone, Radhakrishanan explains how caste system fell from the time based necessity to an unreasonable social obsession. He states that a natural evolution conditioned by the times....the flexibility of the original class system gave way to the rigidity of the castes. The so called Hinduisation of the tribes was a gradual process during which the existing tribes, who were spread all over the peninsula and occupied a much more area than they do now, came in contact with the process of Aryanisation, mostly by way of conflict. Many of the tribes, as dominated classes, found place at the lower orders of the Hindu society. Many pockets even maintained their distinct identity without any caste system, some even till the present day.

The same view is echoed from various corners that the tribal population has been waging a losing battle against the advance of the Aryans since the earliest invasions. Most administrations considered them a source of danger to the outposts of civilisation and in the vicimty of their lands. Many of the rulers adopted a ruthless policy of dominance towards them since they looked at the tribal pockets with suspicion. In this evrionment of mutual mistrust and occasional clash of interest the primitive peoples were exterminated and many more lost their identity in the course of the growth of Hindu civilisation. At the same time some of them accepted the suzerainty of their civilised overlords, and retained their ancestral lands. Basham states:

The Arthashashtra maintains such people as useful in time of war. Many of these tribes came more and more under the influence of Aryan ways, and their tribal cults were undoubtedly the ancestors of many lower Hindu castes of later times... Most of them are now partly civilized and Hinduized but some, though happy folk, knit together by tribal custom into solid, self-supporting and self-sufficient communities, still preserve vestiges of ferocious and barbaric tradition (197).

This passage from tribe to caste, ie, from jana to jati, had political and economic reasons as well. Extension of control over new or the present settlements was hugely important in order to retain economic, social and political power. This sometimes also led to annexing the territory of other kingdoms, or of the atavika rajas, forest-chiefs. As always, conflicts, campaigns and sometimes even wars were necessary, both to annex territory and to enhance income through collecting booty. Tribal lords or the forest-chiefs were subjugated and their societies incorporated into that of the conquerors, supposedly through a process of osmosis but equally likely through some coercion. According to Romila Thapar, "This involved induction into the caste, the families of the chiefs being accorded kshatriya status or, if important enough, accorded a lineage connection through a marriage alliance. However, the rest of the clan generally fell into varying shudra statuses" (422).

This historical and cultural perspective to the origin of the tribals since the invasion of the Aryans, mainly depending upon the works of historians, philosophers, social and literary historians takes cognizance of the vulnerability of the Aryan invasion theory. However, the tribal presence in forests is corroborated not only by the historians but the epics too and the tribal society, though a casteless society, could not remain unaffected by the social caste structures.

Christian missionaries too played a very important part in as far as the tribal question is concerned. The missionaries of various orders and sects carried the message of Christ along with health and education facilities. An observation by Guha sums up the situation, "The soap and the Bible were the twin engines of Europe's cultural conquest. For historical reasons specific to the Raj the soap prevailed over the Bible in our subcontinent" (Ranajit Guha 4-5). Such was the influence of the missionaries on the 'tribal situation' that many colonial anthropologists, including their Indian counterparts, considered them to be not just reliable but also, to an extent, custodians of the tribal heritage (Roycroft 2004), The difference in the achievements of these missionaries is stark- whereas in the mainstream Indian societies the role of the missionaries remained less influential, even though noticeable, in the tribal areas the march of the missionaries has been spectacular. There are many states in the North-East India where the majority of the people are Christians. Directly or indirectly these missionary activities served the larger purposes of the empire.

For various geographical and historical reasons," there was only one part of British India where a policy of non-interference and protection enabled the tribal populations to retain their land and their traditional life-style. In the hill regions of North-east India which enclose the Brahmaputra valley in the shape of an enormous horseshoe, tribes such as Nagas, Mishmis,

Adis, Miris, Apa, Tanis, and Nishis were the sole inhabitants of a vast regions of rugged mountains and narrow valleys into which the peoples settled in the plains of Assam never penetrated" (Haimendorf 35)

Despite collaborations with the non-tribal populations throughout history, the tribal population has remained somewhat same. The tribal society, to its credit, retained the egalitarian spirit of its society (though there are some tribal societies which have caste system). By and large the tribal societies, despite at various stages of hinduisation, are still outside the caste system.

Notes:

1. The transformation in Rey's attitude is remarkable as the term that Roy chose to describe the communities of Chotanagpur was aborigines reclaimers of land and founders of the villages of Chotanagpur His repeated use of the term was indeed to stress the point that these were people who had the greatest claims on the lands of Chotanagpur He saw [tribal] institutions as reminiscences of a glorious past and may have 'contributed not only to the racial make up of the Bengalis, Beharis and Oriya, but also to the social, religious and cultural equipment of these people (158-159).

2. The British government passed an act in 1871 commonly known as the Criminal Tribes Act under which about 150 different castes tribes groups were notified as 'hereditary criminals The crimes included counterfeiting of coins and currency, murder, theft, decosty and housebreaking Many of the tribes

included in the list comprised of those who opposed the expansion of British such as Bhils who had fought the British rule in Khandesh, the Gonds, Marias and Murias of Bastar who participated in militant revolts against the British. Tribes of Chotanagpur such as the Mundas, Oraons, Ho and the Santhals were also included in the list of criminal tribes as they had violently resisted the efforts of the British government to encroach into their lands. Generations of the so called criminal tribes were subjected to humiliation, exploitation, strict surveillance and forced labour.

3. It inevitably brings to mind numerous corresponding examples of exploitation, in Australia, of the members of the stolen generations", "children who were forcibly removed from their homes to be raised in white institutions in an attempt to foster assimilation (Times of India, 2008) Such prejudices among the white settlers led to the removals of children from their families to rid them of their aboriginal characteristics and thus make them like the settlers themselves. What is yet more shocking about the episode that was initiated in 1869 and continued till the 1970s, are the allegations made by the members of the Stolen Generations Alliance of Aborigines which allege that many children were also used as "gunea pigs" for leprosy treatment.

4. It could very well be argued that the process of civilising the tribals is a subversive method well employed to exploit the tribal people and their resources. Stephen Corry explains in a newspaper arucle Loor of Tribal Resources Masquerades As

Progress (2006) how even in the present day Botswana, for example, Gana and Govi Bushmen, have been evicted from their homes in the central Kalahan desert and forced into resettlement camps. Once healthy and self-sufficient, the Bushmen are now dependent on government handouts and are dying from alcoholism and diseases like HIV/AIDS. The government claims this is for development Botsavana's president, Festus Mogal, asked in 1996, "How can you have a stone Age creature continue to exist in the age of computers? If the Bushmen want to survive they must change or otherwise, like the dodo, they will perish." He adds, "As in so many other parts of the world development in Botswana has a hidden agenda, the agenda of extraction and exploitation of natural resources on tribal people's land. Just as adavasis were uprooted and then resettled to make way for the construction of the Narmada dams, the Bushmen have been evicted to make way for diamond mining. Diamonds have been discovered under the bushmen's land and the mining company De Beers holds a mining retention license that allows them to mine at some point in the future."

Works Cited:

Basham, A L The Wonder That Was India. 1967. 3rd ed. New Delhi: Rupa, 1997. Print.

Balfour, Edward G., ed. Enclopedia Asiatica Comprising Indian Subcontinent, Eastern and southern Asia: Commercial, Industrial and Scientific, 1858. 3rd ed. Vol.5. New Delhi: Cosmo, 1976. Print. 9 vols.

Boehmer, Elleke. Colonial and Postcolonial Literature. 1995. New Delhi: OUP, 2006. Print.

Corry, Stephen "Modern Times. Loot of Tribal Resources Masquerades as Progress." The Times of India. 10 April 2006. Print.

Dasgupta, Sangeeta. "Recasting the Oraons and the 'Tribe" Sarat Chandra Roy's Anthology" (132-171) Anthropology in the East Founders of Indian Sociology and Anthropology. Eds. Patricia Uberoi et al. Ranikhet: Permanent Black, 2007. Print.

Dimri, Jaiwanti Images and Representation of the Rural Women: A Study of Selected Novels of Indian Women Writers Shimla IIAS, 2012. Print.

Doniger, Wendy The Hindus An Alternative History New Delhi: Penguin/ Viking 2009 Print

Guha, Ramchandra "Between Anthropology and Literature: The Ethnography of Verrier Elwin" (330-359). Anthropology in the East. Founders of Indian Sociology and Anthropology Eds. Patricia Uberoi et al Ranikhet: Permanent Black, 2007. Print.

Guha, Ranajit. "The Small Voice of History" 1996. Subaltern Studies Ed Shahid Amin and Dipesh Chakrabarty. Vol. IX. New Delhi: OUP, 2005. Print.

Keay, John India A History New Delhi: Grove Press, 2001. Print.

Kipling, Rudyard. Stories of India. Ed Sudhakar Marathe New Delhi: Penguin, 2003 Print.

Marathe, Sudhakar. Introduction. Stories of India. By Rudyard Kipling. Ed Marathe. New Delhi. Penguin, 2003 Print.

McLeod, John. Beginning Postocolonialism. Manchester Manchester UP 2000. Print.

Radhakrishnan, S Indian Philosophy. 1922, OUP, 1998. 2 vols. Print.

Radhakrishna, Meena. Dishonoured by History: Criminal Tribes and British Colonial Policy New Delhi. Orient Longman, 2001. Print.

Ray, Niharranjan Introduction The Tribal Situation in India 1972. Ed. K. Suresh Singh. Shimla. IIAS, 2002 Print.

Ram, Kalpana. "Anthropology as 'Ananthropology' LK. Ananthakrishna Iyer (1861-1937), Colonial Anthropology, and the "Native Anthropologist as Pioneer (64-105) Anthropology in the East Founders of Indian Sociology and Anthropology Eds. Patricia Uberoi et al. Ranikhet Permanent Black, 2007. Print.

Roy, Arundhati The shape of the Beast: Conversation with Arundhati Roy. New Delhi: Penguin/Viking, 2008. Print.

Roycroft, Daniel J. "Capturing Birsa Munda: The Virtuality of a Colonial era Photo- graph." Indian Folklore Research Journal, Vol. 1, No. 4, 2004: 53-68. Print.

Spivak, Gayatri Chakravorty "A Literary Representation of the Subaltern: Mahasweta Devi's 'Stanadayini" (91-134). 1987. Subaltern Studies. Ed. Ranajit Guha. 2nd ed. Vol. V. New Delhi: OUP, 1995. Print.

Spivak, Gayatri Chakravarty. "Discussion: An Afterword on the New Subaltern" (305-335). 2000. Subaltern Studies. Community, Gender and Violence. Eds. Partha and Pradeep Jeganathan. Vol. XI. New Delhi: Permanent Black, 2009. Print.

Tharoor, Shashi India: From Midnight to Millenium. New Delhi: Penguin, 1997. Print.

Thapar, Romila. Early India: From the Origins to AD 1300. New Delhi: Penguin, 2002. Print.

The Times of India. "Aboriginal Kids Used as Guinea Pigs in Australia? 16 April 2008. Print.

Chapter - 3

Violence & Hype-money in the Subaltern Legacy

"Domination and inequities of power and wealth are perennial facts of human society".

Edward W. Said
Culture and Imperialism

The exploitation of human beings and their resources by fellow human beings has been a 'perennial truth that mankind has known since time immemorial. It is this exploitation of one by the other and the following resistance, that has influenced the course of human history and that constitutes the most part of history. Empires were built in order to channelise and legitimise it and wars were fought in order to gain control over other's resources. If exploitation is an inherent trait in human beings, so is resistance to it.

The tribal world has faced all the possible agents of exploitation, ranging from the ones representing the empire to the ones that are present within their own communities. Afterall, the tribai world need not be romanticised for it too has many of its own who lose no opportunity in looting the resources of their own people. The agents of exploitation that will be studied here, as depicted in many of the major novels, vary from the imperial British government to the present democracy of the Republic of India; to the other agents of the state such as the officials, development machinery and the tribal people themselves.

As has been argued in the preceding chapter, it was with the arrival of the British in India that the word 'tribe' was used for the first time for those who dwelled in the forest. Also, it was with their successive policies that led to the massive exploitation and alienation of the tribals, and it has also been seen that the tribals rose in one rebellion after another against the colonial power. The structure of power in the British era has been defined by Ranajit Guha as:

In colonial India.. power simply stood for a series of inequalities between the rulers and the ruled as well as between classes, strata and individuals among the latter themselves...these unequal relationships,.....may all be said to have derived from a general relation- that of Dominance (D) and Subordination (S). These two terms imply each other: it is not possible to think of D without S and vice versa.

General Configuration of Power

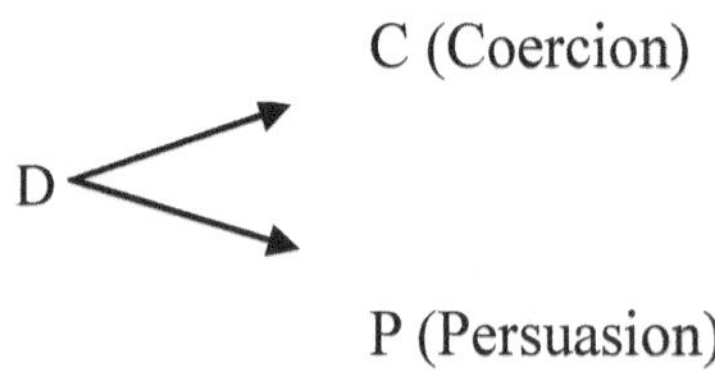

Power (D/S)

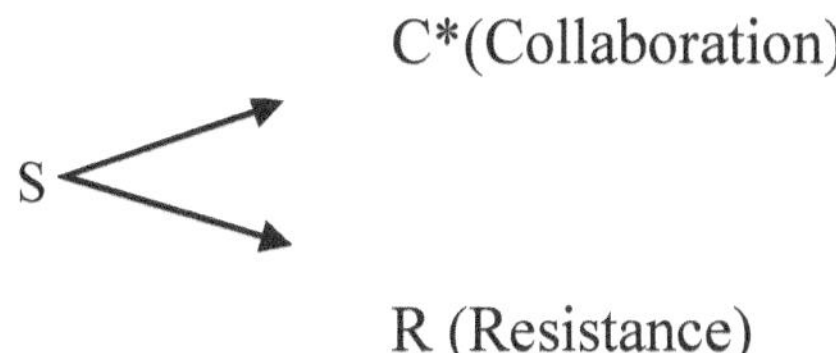

...while D and Simply each other logically and the implication applies to all cases where an authority structure can be legitimately defined in those terms... mutual implication of C and P or of C and R is true only under given conditions [and thus exists] contingently (Guha 1989: 229).*

History of colonial India is about indomitable power and the resistance that it evoked from throughout the subcontinent. The relation of power that the imperial government had with the natives depended not just on the objectives and the intentions of the rulers but also on the standing of the section of the natives in the national society. The indigenous people or the adivasis eventually became the softest targets of the imperial government for various reasons. Their habitat was abundant in natural resources and the imperial power had no intentions of allowing it to be in the hands of those who had no control on its being snatched away. The government was quick to see the vast economic possibilities such sources provided for the government to carry out several of its projects regarding defence, trade and transportation. Secondly, they could be invaluable to the imperial cause in terms of human labour. Kaushik Ghosh traces how the tribals of Chotanagpur area were identified as 'excellent labourers' who could be 'utilized as coolies' (Ghosh 9). Large numbers of labourers from Chotanagpur and other tribal areas were transported to tea estates in Assam and Darjeeling. Thirdly, their suffering could not arouse protest from the mainstream native society as for them they were relatively barbaric and the attempt of the colonial masters to civilise the forest dwellers should have to be appreciated even if it caused the 'barbarians' some inconvenience.

According to Guha, it is on the 'contingency of power relations arising from the reciprocity of C and Pin D and that of C and R in S... such contingency must be recognised as the site where 'human passion mediates the concept of power and turns it into a history of dominance and subordination (230).

Prior to any textual exegesis, it would be appropriate to see the first major step of the non-tribal world that rendered them vulnerable and deprived them of their own resources and made their exploitation not just easier but also almost inevitable. The forest resources began to be identified by the British as indispensable to their larger cause globally. Though they had begun to intrude into the tribal tracts throughout rid India through contractors, zamindars, the police and the missionaries (though they were independent in their own sense, yet were seen by many as somehow furthering the cause of the aliens), it was the Indian Forest Act VII (1878) which was indeed the culmination of various attempts of the British to consolidate and legalise the forests as the property of the state. Though various initiatives regarding land 'reforms' and revenue systems had already antagonised farmers in various parts of the country, it was this act of 1878 that proved to be almost fatal for the tribal population.

The Indian Forest Act VII 1878, classified forests into Reserved, Protected, and Village Forests, and provided the necessary laws and rules for establishing and handling an absolute state monopoly on forests (Linkenback 127). The communities for whom the forests meant not just their habitat but also a symbol of their cultural identity, such an act provided a death knell and a reason for all the anguish, which upon the gradual implementation led to rebellion. The Act undermined the role of forest for the tribals. It was outright exploitation.

The importance of forest has been understood by human beings for quite a long time now. It is this anxiety about the misuse and exploitation of forest resources that Aldous Huxlery writes about as:

In politics we have so firm a faith in the manifestly unknowable future that we are prepared to sacrifice millions of lives to an opium smokers' dream of Utopia or world dominion of perpetual security. But where natural resources are concerned we sacrifice a pretty accurately predictable future to present greeds. We know for example that if we abuse the soil and massacre our forests our children will lack timber and see their uplands eroded, their valleys swept by floods. Nevertheless, we continue to abuse the soil and massacre the forests. In a word, we immolate the present to the future in those complex affairs where fore-thought is impossible, but in relatively simple affairs of Nature, where we know quite well what is likely to happen, we immolate the future to the present (Sagreiya 1967: 1).

This worry of the civilian society about its natural resources and the happiness of its future generations led the governments into formulating forest policies. This protection of forests by governments has caused humankind more benefit than loss. However, there is one section of Indian population that became a loser right from the onset. It is the tribal population for whom the forests were their home, their environment and an important constituent of their identity as Vinita Damodaran states, "The importance of the forest economy to many local communities of the region [Chotanagpur] in the nineteenth century can not be underestimated" (2005).

Some regulations of the forest act of 1878 played havoc with the normal lives of the tribal population. One was: 'The sole object of administering state forests is in public benefit. In general the constitution and preservation of a forest involve the regulation of rights and the restriction of privileges of the user of the forest by the neighboring population (Sagreiya 11).

This hit at the very root of the practices on which tribal lives were sustained. It is a fact that the needs of the tribals are easily met by the forest cover that surrounds their habitation since their needs are not on the proportion of those of the mainstream society with its factories, railways, ship industries, fuel-oriented industries, constructions and so on. Tribal societies are not known to have destroyed large areas of forests. It is done by the large settlements of the mainstream societies in new areas who seek more fertile soil for cultivation.

The phrase- 'the sole object with which state forests are administered is public benefit' is ambiguous since it does not mention 'which public'? Of course, the implication, however, is that this benefit is made accessible to the public of the empire that lived in its cities and towns, not just in India but also in the UK and elsewhere in the empire. The dearest cost was paid by the public that lived in or around those forests who are culturally inclined anyway to protect the forests since it meant so much to them. This process initiated by the empire-building machinery was used to the maximum to exploit the tribal population thereafter.

The Act also had certain other clauses which provided a smokescreen to its exploitative nature. Ordinarily, if a demand for agricultural land arises and can be met from a forest alone it should be conceded without hesitation, subject to a few conditions such as honeycombing of a valuable forest by patches of cultivation should not be allowed and cultivation must be permanent and must not be allowed to extend so as to encroach upon the minimum area of forest that is needed to meet the reasonable forest requirement, present and prospective.

I

One of the most suitable examples of imperial exploitation and the resistance following it is depicted in Birenndra Kumar Bhattacharya's Mrityunjaya. This Assamese novel, written decades after the uprising during the Quit India movement of 1942 narrates in vivid detail the way the people responded to the spirit of this movement. It is not a novel about the tribal issues in particular but it showcases how the tribal people join the others around them with only one goal in mind and that is the freedom of their motherland from the clutches of imperial Britain.

The novel describes in detail how a society of peace- loving people, in response to extraordinary situations, is disillusioned with non-violence and in order to achieve ends such as peace and freedom takes to violent means, much against its wishes. The volunteers are in reality followers of Mahatma Gandhi but resort to violent means in order to ignite the fading momentum of the revolution. They understand too well by now the design of the imperial government. Gosain's contemplation of the imperial design reflects the depth of their understanding of the problem and its possible solutions:

His father had never been able to understand why the British had established/laid railway lines all across Assam. They set up the railways to supply away their oil, coal and tea to the big markets and to make huge profits out of this business. By earning this profit the British became richer and the Assamese villagers became poorer. The local king

122

of Mayang, Raja Baneshwar became the subject of the Queen of London the empress of an empire on which the sun never set. It is by the poor understanding of this intrigue in the earlier stages that the situation has come to this.... Also he felt embarrassed that his forefathers were so naive (Mrityunjay 160).

Here it would not be out of context to mention the article of the New York Times (1901), which has been discussed in the beginning, where the foreign correspondent reporting from Simla writes about the Indian Viceroy, Lord Curzon's trip to the hilly tracks of the north east of India, which happens to be the location in which the novel is set. The article reads.

The whole country, indeed, is rich to a degree, but at present remains in an almost primitive condition owing to the difficulty of communication. Until the railway has been brought to these parts there can be little or no real development, and the making of a railway is a difficult matter, though not insuperably so. A large number of separate hilly ranges have to be crossed at right angles, and such a line would therefore be a most expensive one to construct. But there can be little doubt that such a line will be made before long, and the prospects of its early construction have been immensely improved now that Lord Curzon has seen the country for himself.

This underlines the exploitation of the masses and their resources that cause the people to rise in unison against the atrocities of the empire in the name of 'real development. This is in line with the efforts of the empire builders that had gone on in most parts of the world, in many places much before it took roots in the Indian subcontinent. Niall Ferguson recounts a satire from the official Matabeleland campaign souvenir, published on the fortieth anniversary of that one sided conflict by the British to conquer the Matabele 'savages' in Africa (1893) where 1500 Matabele soldiers were wiped out with the help of the Maxim gun by incurring a casualty of just four invaders out of a total of 700. It reads:

Onward Chartered soldiers, on to the heathen lands,
Prayer books in your pockets, rifles in your hands.
Take the glorious tidings where trade can be done,
Spread the peaceful gospel- with a Maxim gun. (226)

The central action of the novel (Mrityunjaya) involves the preparations leading to the derailing of the train bringing in troops and ammunition. The success of the plan (which indeed they achieved) would halt the crushing of the revolutionaries. In addition to fighting against the imperial power, the people also try to break old barriers amongst themselves. Dimi is the indomitable Garo woman who participates fully in the struggle. Not only she but her entire village stands up along with the revolutionaries and contributes to the national struggle.

When Gosainjee asks Dimi to prepare tea, his colleague Ashina Konwar refuses to have tea made by the tribal Dimi since they all belong to the upper Hindu castes. That is when Gosainjee echoes the modern sentiments by linking them to the rich and unbiased cultural heritage of India as he tells Konwar, "Even Lord Rama had food from the hands of Guha Chandala, What happened?" (102)

Bhibhi Ram, another colleague gave a similar reply, "If Lord Krishna can have food in the house of Kubja Malin and if Sita can have food from the hands of demons in the Ashok Van then how will we pollute our caste by having food from the hands of Dimi" (102)

The revolutionaries are very clear about the goals of their struggle. They know that exploitation is not just due to the imperial government but also by the other indigenous factors which will stay even after the empire is forced out. The novel ends with due acknowledgement of the efforts of none other than Dimi, the tribal woman when Gosawinin exclaims to Anupama, "Something has happened in this country. I now feel it properly. Otherwise why should the mind of even this Garo woman, the tribal Dimi turn revolutionary" (280)?

Though she expresses her surprise that in the struggle of the people of Assam for the independence of the country even a tribal woman should be so involved, it is nonetheless in the praise of Dimi's tireless effort in not just sacrificing her own happiness for nation's independence but also rallying her community around. The community also rises to the occasion knowing they would lose everything in the process. Anupama finally tells Gosainin, "Today all the downtrodden races of the world are struggling for independence then why not these people" (280)?

The chain of acts of exploitation does not, however, end with the passing away of the empire. The modern texts, written even about the post-independence situation and democracy, show that the tribal people are still subjected not onlt to exploitation at the hands of state officials, but also by the objectives of the state, mostly in the name of development. The uprooting and rehabilitation of the tribal people in large numbers to make way for the building of dams, projects and other such developmental programmes is a very common reality of post-independent India.

Gopinath Mohanty's Oriya classic *Paraja* (1945) is an example of how the agents of the state machinery (despite being Indians) show little concern for the pain of tribals. Paraja is a tragic tale of a family belonging to a tribe by the name of Paraja, living in the forest tracks of Koraput in Orissa. The novel narrates the struggle of a family against all odds. It is a story of suppression and exploitation of a tribal family and their finally falling victim to the vicious trap. The interesting thing discussed in the novel is that the mainstream world is not solely blamed for the ills and suffering of the tribal people. It does not romanticise the situation.

The novel is rooted in reality and helps unveil the reality of human nature. The main theme of the novel is exploitation and suffering. The exploitation and the suffering caused by it as shown in the novel are appalling for two reasons, this colossal damage is caused by petty reasons and it goes on till it finally destroys Sukru Jant and his entire family. Also, it depicts the vulnerability of the tribal people as such minor intrigues can shatter their entire world. Secondly, the novel shows that agents of exploitation are not just from the outside, but from within the tribal world.

Paraja is the story of Sukru Jani and his two sons Mandia Jani and Tikra Jani. Along with them a very crucial role is played by Sukru Jani's daughters, Jili and Bili. This family belongs to Paraja tribe. The ambitious and hard working Sukru Jani wants to increase his cultivable land for which he has to clear a patch of forest. He bribes the forest Guard and obtains permission. Meanwhile the forest guard one evening sees his elder daughter Jili having a bath in the river and then sends a message to Sukru Jani to send his daughter over to him. Sukru Jani refuses to part with his daughter's honour.

This leads to the beginning of all the troubles. The vindictive Guard takes revenge and Sukru Jani is punished for clearing the patch of forest. Then begins the story of suffering under debt, legal punishment and Sukru Jani and his elder son Mandia Jani become bonded labourer (goti) of the money lender Sahukar Bisoi. In this trapping some of the tribal cousins of Sukru Jani play a very vicious role. This brings to the fore the point that the innocent and all fearing tribals are not just exploited by the people from the mainstream outside society who act as the agents of oppression but are also exploited by the members of their own community or tribe. This presents a very realistic view of the situation and shows the tribals as real-human beings like the rest of the humanity.

Paraja is extraordinary in so far as Sukru Jani and his family fall from one sorrow to another. The exploitation baton passes from the Forest Guard to Sahukar Bisoi who is relentless in his routing the family. All the males of the family become his gotis and he marries the elder daughter Jili, which is still another form of dominance. Jili and Bili had earlier been lured by prostitution along with heing construction labourers. The family only show the final resistance when Sukru Jani and his sons hack the Sahukar with their axes and then run to surrender to the police. This novel gives a true account of the suffering of the tribal society whose initial suffering led to shock and dismay and subsequent exploitation to resentment and ultimately violence.

The novel inevitably draws comparison with the African writer Chinua Achebe's Things Fall Apart which was published in 1958. The destiny of the Paraju tribe in Koraput seems to be shared in equal measure by that of Umuofia in Africa, i.e., how a primitive community is disintegrated under the impact of an alien force, that of a new faith, a new power structure that has both a new value system and manifold strength. The Paraja family of Sukru Jani, his wife, two sons and two daughters had enjoyed relative prosperity under the barter system before they became a part of a 'story of shattered dreams (Mahapatra 1992). Okonkwo too was a prosperous and a proud farmer before a series of events led to his humiliation when his head was shaved in the police station. The righteously proud protagonists of these novels found it beyond their capacity to adapt to a hostile system that was determined not just to defeat them eventually but to demoralize them, and to 'colonize' them.

Similar stories of such nature across two different continents, confirm the universal nature of attempts of a superior power system to dominate and exploit a materially inferior society. The members of the suffering society were awe struck at the mechanism of the exploiter, which intentionally or otherwise, moved through police stations, courts and other departments. When the oppressed was pushed to the wall, he (in the form of a Sukru Jani or an Okonkwo) reacted in the only manner that he thought was still open to him violence. Both the novels end with extreme violence, the only means that the exploiter had left the oppressed with.

Government machinery responsible for bringing about a change and development is another of such agents which, even though with noble intentions, more often than not end up disturbing the very fabric of the tribal society.

A very prominent author who has tirelessly worked for the cause of the tribal people is Mahasweta Devi. It is primarily through her fiction that we see the real and the grim reality of the tribal people. Mahasweta Devi's Rudali is a seminal text in terms of the discussion' of the exploited, the weak, the marginalised and the subaltern. It is also about the degradation of womanhood which is exploited to the hilt by those in the position of power. Anjum Katyal wrtites, "Set against this exploitative system is the issue of survival. Rudali is about... "how to survive' "bread and mouth'. It is very important in my story. The whole system is exposed through this," says Mahasweta Devi [in an interview in Calcutta on 26.5.93]. The text reveals the various strategies of survival employed by the subaltern individually and as a community" (9).

The central figure of the novel is Sanichari who is a part of a community perpetually dominated and exploited by the more powerful Rajput community. She is rendered helpless by the death of her husband. There are many others like her in her low caste ganju community. They have only two options left for survival; one is prostitution and the other is to become a professional funeral wailer at a rich landlord's death, thus the term 'rudali'. Dulan is a male from her community who works as a guide and a mentor to her. Raudali is a reality based tragic tale of struggle of the oppressed classes just to survive when living itself is no less than a calamity.

Dulan once told them the history of their sufferings:

The Rajputs were warriors in the army of the raja of Chotanagpur. About two hundred years ago, in protest against the cruel oppression practised against them, the kol tribals revolted. The raja immediately sent his army to put down the uprising. Even after the rebellion was suppressed, the Rajput warriors' aggression was not satiated. They went on a rampage, killing innocent tribals and burning down villages. So Harda and Donka Munda started sharpening their arrows, and a fresh tribal uprising was imminent. Then the raja sent his Rajput sardars into the sparsely populated region. He told them, take as much land as is covered by throwing your swords in the air. Start at sunrise and carry on till sundown. There are seven of you. Claim as much land as you can in this way then live off it (73).

Thus the Rajputs increased their power from time to time and the poor lower castes and the tribals were reduced to being bonded labourers in their estates. The landlords were called malik mahajans and they were reckless in not only socio-economic exploitation of the dominated classes but also in their sexual exploitation.

There was a large number of illegitimate children that the landlords begot off the working women only to be dumped and disclaimed thereafter.

Many of the helpless women such as Sanicharı had no choice but to join prostitution as their means of survival. Another lucrative means of survival was to be a funeral wailer at the death of a rich landlord. This reflects the vanity and hollowness of the hegemonic groups as they want to show off to their peers by organising a more impressive funeral than those of the others. The Rudalis charged different amounts of money for different duties rendered during the funeral. All the wailers were whores, especially the older ones

The novel is remarkable for the adaptability of the exploited women. Instead of being used by the system, they appropriate the system to suit their needs which is their survival. It is rightly said in the novel, "Let a few whores from the bazaar come to their funerals. It is the malik mahajans who have turned them into whores, ruined them then kicked them out, is it not so? Don't weight right and wrong so much. Leave that kind of thing to the rich. They understand it better. We understand hunger" (90).

The consistent theme of hunger is prevalent in other texts as well Pratibha Ray's Aadibhoomi which mentions the bonda tribe's tug of war against hunger. There is a question that haunts the minds of young Bonda men, "Which is greater hunger or your lover?" The answer invariabily is, "Hunger is greater than the lover. Hunger is greater than God"(24).

Towards the end of Rudali we are made familiar with the uncomfortable truth as to how not just Sanichari has mastered the art of survival but also how the others of her community have joined her. Not just that, she also initiates others into it. There was an eager bustle among the whores. The young ones asked, 'and us?' Sanichari replied, "All of you come. When you grow old you shall have to do this anyway, so while I am around let me initiate you" (91).

The exploitation of the tribal people in the name of development and even otherwise shall have to be given sufficient attention if the entire country is to strive towards more development along with equality, For this, exploitation has to be checked on the one side and tribal people can be empowered with education ducation and representation in the society's decision making bodies on the other hand. Also, literature about such issues deserves more attention since it reflects the truth of their reality.

There has been an ongoing debate in the context of the tribal population all over the world, that is, whether they should be left 'undisturbed' or brought into the 'mainstream". The views on this subject have often varied drastically from each other. in this context literature may be extremely helpful to acquaint the reader with the possibility of the either.

Pratibha Ray's novel *Adibhoomi* (1993) is a detailed 'cultural biography of the Bonda tribe living in the almost inaccessible mountains of Koraput in Orissa. The tribe has a total population of around five thousand and the state government is keen to not just save them from extinction but also to develop them so that they can be included in the mainstream society. All the 'Bondadesh' comprises of a total of thirty two villages and each village has its own nayak who is the headman of the village. They call their god Patkhamba Mahaprabhu. A peculiar trait of these people is that they call themselves Remo meaning "human' while the other people living in the lower regions call them bonda-signifying not just the tribe they belong to but condemning them as naked and uncivilised

The author explains the peculiar attitude of the bondas towards life. A Bonda does not know his age, nor the history of his parents. He does not know his traditions but only that he is a descendant of a warrior class who, hiding away from civilisation and have been surviving by struggling with nature. He does not know the meaning of forgiveness and rivalry and crime have only one punishment - Death. The author does not exaggerate when she says that nature means everything to a Bonda and they all are the children of nature and they are like nature- open, clear, hard and naked. They don't know lies or fraud and apart from a bonda they do not trust anyone. A bonda suspects others might defeat or kill him and that is why he has become violent and suspicious. On that hill of the Khariput block exists the bondadesh where the line between civilisation and primitivism is not blurred but clearly demarcated in terms of time and geography.

After a study of some of the important texts based on the tribal population, one comes to understand the effect 'representation' can have on their life and destiny. In Aadibhoomi the author does not glorify the characteristics of the bonda tribesmen. She does not condemn them either, She, like an artist, narrates the matter of fact story line, while drawing attention to the issues around them. She avoids a judgmental stand and guides one through, like an observer and a presenter. The credit which goes to her due to such a portrayal is that the author attempts to find out, through research in the particular field, the possible reasons and backgrounds, which, to a large degree explain the behavior of the characters in the novel. Where the British government condemned the tribals in general and even framed them perpetually through the Criminal Tribes Act of 1871, modern day authors take special care to visit the cultural history of the people in question.

Pratibha Ray takes pains in explaining why bonda society is violent and seemingly unforgiving. It is a society that is democratic in the true sense and where no one is poor or an orphan. It goes back to unmarked time when the queen of Chakrakot took refuge in the bondadesh having lost her king husband to the enemies and her own territory to the betrayal of the minister. Bondas accepted the Bundi Maharani as their mother and she trained them in warfare in case of an attack on their sovereignty. Even a five year old bonda was trained. The author suggests that it was this anxiety of the enemy attack which kept them ever prepared for war. Also the bondas were suspicious of the four warriors, who had accompanied the maharani, of treachery.

With the passage of time, Bundi maharani and her warriors entered the bonda society permanently and the bonda society was divided into four different departments. nayak (the headman or the mukhiya), sisa (the priest or the pujari), kirsani (warrior) and dhangra manjhi (behra). It is since then the munda society does not take any chance and safeguard their independence fiercely. They get suspicious of anyone, fearing that in the manner of the treachery of the maharani's minister, someone's individual ambition might turn them into slaves. The author observes, "The seeds of suspicion have been germinating in the minds of bondas since that day. God knows, the betrayal in the blood of the minister of Bundi Maharani might erupt in some or the other bonda. After all, what is so strange about betrayal in order to become the king of the independent bondas" (*Adibhoomi* 21).

In order to safeguard their own way of life and their independence, the bonda tribe has taken a refuge in the inhospitable terrain. Such terrain is probably responsible for enabling the Mundas to lead a secure and an undisturbed life. It was the unpredictability and the hostility that haunted those contours that probably prevented less equipped and inadequately motivated entrepreneurs from the 'outside' from 'exploring' the bondadesh for a long period. This was a necessarily impenetrable exterior that the bondas needed to lead their own way of life. The real threat to their way of life arose only when the fast developing world of outside began to spread its tentacles far and wide and the tribals began to fight a losing battle right from the beginning.

Javeed Alam explains the reasons for the behaviour of the tribals, which at times, we may find unreasonable. Alarm brings to our notice an interesting anecdote from Jharkhand:

In a remote inaccessible village (in Jharkhand) where the people (almost all tribals) had to walk many miles for their first contact with what we call civilization to sell what they collect from the forests, the government decided to provide this village with a road. As the survey party reached the area, it met with resistance and was driven off. The survey team came back after a while with some police protection and after a somewhat riotous encounter with the tribals it had to withdraw once again. Later on, one curious engineer in the survey team, who was feeling very intrigued with this refusal to have a road, took it upon himself to move in personally to have a dialogue regarding this intransigence of the villagers... The villagers did not want a road because with it will come the merchant and the trader for the forest products and the other merchandise. Soon the police will follow to beat them up and arrest them because resistance between the traders and the local people is bound to emerge against exploitation and brutal oppression.

The villagers said that what they will end up in is the raj of the Dikku (11).

Alam argues that, "The tribal languages have a feature which is an important reflection on their life. Their languages do not contain words of abuse. So what happens when the tribal confronts the constant presence of a dikku, who is abuse personified?" (12). Therefore it is inevitable that the hapless tribal gives vent to his ange in other forms. According to Alam, "Another helpless victim of brutal exploitation, Harijan, as he withdraws into his own world, can be extremely abusive and this helps him in renewing himself as a human being everyday to go on living life. The tribal can not even do that. He is simply baffled and remains baffled. All he can do is to say that the other person is a dikku. Points are reached in his life when he can not accumulate any more. Given the egalitarian nature of tribal solidarity and the unifromity of the similar experience by all, what very often happens is a collective eruption of violence against the Dikku who also personifies the predatory nature of the State for the tribals. We, like the English in the nineteenth century, are taken back by this because the point at which eruption occurs is not provocative enough for us to see the necessity of such violence" (Alam 12).

Pratibha Ray, through Adibhoomi, gives a detailed view of the life of the bonda tribe. Some of the characteristics are egalitarianism, socio-economic equality, lack of caste system and social camaraderie. Egalitarianism is one the foundations of the bonda society. The 'election' in the bonda villages for the post of nayak is an interesting episode since one is generally pushed into it by the fellow tribesmen. Though the nayak is always proud of his position, he is expected to accept the post saying a repeated na na, ie, attempting to decline the offer modestly. When Baghbindu's name was proposed for the post of nayak he protested, "I don't want to be the nayak. There's no profit, only loss. I will be dragged all over- Khariput- Malkangiri- Koraput" (213). Baghbindu compares it with the elections in the mainstream society which he had learnt from the imprisoned criminals who were his mates in the jail. He remembers, "The leaders are virtuous, religious and calm since they do not indulge themselves in committing murders and dacoity as they have others to do it for them" (214). After Baghbindu became the nayak, a separate room was built for him in the house for the period and as per the custom special care was taken to make the house indistinguishable from the rest of the houses so that all the houses looked the same.

Economic and social equality is another principle upon which the tribal society of the bondas has existed ever since. But after contact with the outside world the tribal world began to lose some of its virtues while incorporating the characteristics of the outsiders. After the completion of the first residential quarters of the Indira Awas Yojna, the Block Development Officer (BDO) announces to the bonda crowd, "Bonda brothers, listen. The government has built houses for you. You will be able to live there peacefully and without any diseases. But for the time being we only have eight houses ready. Each house has cost the government twenty five thousand rupees. Eight families can move in. More houses will follow. The houses will be alloted to the poor first. Those who are the poorest raise your hands" (393).

Baghbindu, the nayak of Mudlipada, the man who was 'educated' since he had spent fourteen years in prison after man slaughter, stood up and said, "There are no poor amongst us. We are all equal. We don't want government houses. Go away. We don't care for your committee." The BDO folded his hands and pleaded, "Tomorrow some of you should be living in those houses. The delegation should see that the bondas have been civilized. After that you may leave them. You will be paid" (393).

Soon a whole lot of them stake claim to the quarters citing how poor they were. Baghbindu, the nayak, too pleaded for a house for his son. None of them forgot to remind the BDO that they should stay in those houses only so long as they are paid for it. The author laments, "Mud houses and tin houses the bonda tribe has divided into two parts from today- rich and poor" (394).

A coherent society was another tenet of the bonda society. When the authorities built an orphanage, bondas were at a loss to understand why such things were ever needed. They protested that there was no orphan in bondadesh, "If the child is fatherless his mother looks after him. If our child does not have a mother then some uncle or the other villagers take care of him. If there is none the Patkhamba Mahaprabhu is there. But there is no orphan among us" (437).

Corresponding to the fictional reality in Adibhoomi, Piyush Mankad, a former civil servant, narrates an interesting tale of the 1960s when the Madhya Pradesh government took numerous steps to modernise its tribal population:

> *As a part of bringing modernity and progress to these supposedly backward sections of the society, brick and mortar houses were built for them as a pilot project in the Betul district...which were to replace the traditional huts which were made of bamboo, plastered with mud, covered with thatch on the sloping roofs, and often decorated with beautiful tribal drawings and motifs. A good deal of money was spent and it was handed over to the tribals with much political fanfare, satisfied for having done something good for these 'ignorant, poor people' Three months down the line, to their utter disbelief, the team found that the tribals still continued to live in their traditional thatch roof huts, and were using the newly built houses to keep their beloved livestock.... The tribal people just could not sleep in those brick and mortar houses, or use the strange toilets, or cook in the confined kitchens, and so what better use of the new houses then to utilise them to keep their precious cattle? (2009).*

Aadibhoomi is not just a cultural and biographical representation of the bondas, as has been discussed earlier, it is the story of the efforts of the development process initiated by the nation state, in order to bring all its people to a common ground of development. The condition on ground was dismal. Many project officers had joined and left. After a long time the one 'leader babu' who took it upon himself to 'extend the government's helping hand to the bondas effectively was Sitanath Sahu. He found out that eight schools in bondadesh had been running since 1960, the staff was being paid regularly when there were no school buildings and students on ground.

Sitanath Sahu began by introducing to the tribals the subsidies in terms of seeds and agricultural loans in order to grow high yielding crops. He also encouraged the men and women to seek employment in the project office. Adibari, Sombari and Mangli were the first bonda women to discard traditonal cloth piece and wear a sari. He began to send the children to school. Adibari was the first one to be photographed, and that too in sari and printed in the newspaper. He tried to overcome the sloth of the bonda men by trying to invoke in them a feeling of competition in terms of agricultural produce. He made them aware of the comforts that money can buy and how best they could earn it.

The next project officer Shiv Vishwal was the opposite of Sitanath who had been transferred for making the bondas habitual of dependency on government handouts. Vishwal was appointed to the Khariput block as a punishment for having been accused of a financial scam. Whereas Sitanath taught bondas to be polite, Vishwal had already applied for an arms lincence. He discontinued the services of the women appointed by Sitanath, the ones who had pioneered the initiative of joining the project services. Sewing machines were ordered. New road was to be built so that all the officers could reach bondadesh. Bonda Swayamsevak Sangh and Bonda Development Agency were established. All these 'developmental' measures led to a greater influx of government and private contractors into bondadesh.

Indira Awas Yojna was one of the most ambitious schemes of the department. As mentioned earlier, lakhs of rupees had been spent on the quarters for the poor bonda' who could not afford decent and clean housing. The author takes us through what happened to the houses within a year as, "Half of those houses had begun to develop cracks and the plaster had mostly fallen off. They were then hurriedly repaired in order to get them ready for inspection" (461). Later Somra lost his pregnant sister and Adibari's disabled sister when the house constructed under the Indira Awas Yojana collapsed at night. Somra, like any unsuspecting bonda consoled himself that their time had come though he could not help wondering over what the schoolmaster Tripathi ji had said, "How could it collapse within less than a year? Powerful storms couldn't harm the mud huts with thatched roofs how could the Indira Awas Yojna house wall collapse and the tin roofs fly away" (484)?

Ray thus represents the naïve and unsuspecting tribals vis-à-vis the corrupt officials of the state and their private companions. The author sums up the anxiety of the government officials about the 'condition' of the bonda tribe in these words:

Drought has caused serious shortage of water. If immediate action is not taken, not just the vegetation, even people will die. Other people's death is a separate issue. But even if one of the total five thousand bondas dies of famine, there will be furore in the Lok Sabha and the Rajya Sabha. The endangered bonda tribe survives only in these hills. It is due to these that the name of Orissa and the bonda tribe exist on the international sociological and anthropological maps. We get so many tourists, researchers and photographers from all over the world. Their extinction will be a serious loss to the educationists, journalists, film-makers, painters and artists. The [state] government [Orissa] will be the worst hit. On what pretext will it ask for the sanctions of grant from the central government? Who will they exhibit in the national darbar (345)?

Development of the tribals and other backward areas is not just a matter of choice for the state but also a compulsion. But while carrying out various schemes, care should be taken to safeguard the virtues of a culture and it should be ensured that < no exploitation of the supposed beneficiaries takes place. Soma Mudali is still hopeful the bondadesh will not be gripped by the clutches of civilisation and that the bonda will remain a bonda. The government will not be able to run its writ in their land. Such suspicion about the government agencies in the minds of the tribesmen is both due to ignorance and unwillingness to change and also because of their earlier bitter experiences with the agents of civilisation.

Ray elaborates how bondadesh became a hunting ground for the exploiters from the outside and how many of them were wrongly indicted and how on various occasions their women folk were molested. Such exploitation is not simply accepted by the bonda men though there is not much they can really do. Their anguish is epitomized by an incident when Somara shouted at the policemen and the local MLA's brother-in-law:

You men of the contractor and the MLA have looted our hill. Should we continue to tolerate? First you instigated our women to wear sari and then finally deserted them in the bazaar of Jaipur. We tolerated. You looted the hill, you looted our forests and you looted the government money in our name. Even then we tolerated. Now you have looted the honour of our women. We shall not tolerate. You have cut down all our forests. You indeed rendered all of us naked. Today we shall talk to the MLA. We shall talk to the government (482).

The following incident encapsulates the irony of fate of the bonda tribals, and to some extent, of most of the tribals struggling with their confrontation with civilization. A government delegation, on a visit to bondadesh to find out the pace of development and the prevailing conditions of the tribal people, becomes a tool of manipulation by the interpretors:

The head of the delegation- "Is there any bonded labour in your village?"
The interpreter put the question to the bonda gathering.
"We all are bonded labourer!" replied Katu on the behalf of the bondas.

"None of us are bonded labourers," interpreted Tank Khemandi to the officials.

"Good good. Send your children to school. You will be given free books. Teachers will guide you. You have eight schools in your area. Gandhi and Nehru were also children like you. Give up wine and violence. Become human beings."

Pondu Hantal interpreted to the public.

How can you send your children to study when there are no school buildings? There is only hatred. That's why my son Somra went to a far off school. He was looked down upon for being a non-Aryan; tribal. Arya children set themselves on fire and protested against us non-Aryans. College closed and my son returned without becoming an Aryan. Now he hates us and he hates you all. The condition of all our children is the same. Where will they study? How can these people ask us to stop drinking wine when all the project officers drink our own wine (397)?

Obviously, the crowd was baffled.

Before anyone in the crowd would shoot an arrow on the delegation the project officials offered the interpreters a few bundles of bidi saying that the sahibs were proceeding for lunch and assured the delegation, "Bondas are excited. This is how they express their immense joy. They are even calling names and exulting that their children are receiving fine education" (398). The perplexed members nodded. The government will not be able to understand the helplessness of the officials and the ill fortune of the tribals.

In addition to the values of the Bonda tribe the author also brings to light some of their shortcomings and even vices. One of central characters of the novel Baghbindu, comes to represent his tribe in terms of their pattern of behaviour and values. Since a bonda boy is married to an elder woman, sometimes twice his age so that she can look after the household and help him lead a comfortable life. It reveals how women in the bonda society are subjected to passive exploitation. Baghbindu is no different. When his wife Budei Toki becomes old, he deserts her since she can no longer work or even gratify his sexual urge. When she comes to know of his intention of getting a second wife, she, acutely aware of her status in the bonda society, accepts to live along with her co-wife in the same house. But Baghbindu did not want the liability of an ageing wife and therefore decided to divorce her. He said in the presence of her father and brother, "Go to your father's house. You can not give me any more pleasure. You won't let me live peacfully with Chhotli (younger wife). I therefore divorce you" (252). He split the leaves of piri grass into two - [a custom of formalising the divorce process in the bonda society]. The author notes, "Budei can no longer live here! She felt like a flame, doused by cold water. Accepting the bonda custom, she shut her mouth, held her tears and walked out of her house. She did not ask even once who else she could belong to at this age? Who will feed me? How will I live" (252)?

The violent nature of the Bonda men is quite well portrayed. Many situations, where fatal consequence is somehow avoided, become almost humourous. When an epidemic spread in bondadesh, bondas' first attempt was to prevent any doctors from reaching their villages since that would further incur the wrath of the already unhappy devta. Baghbindu suggested, "I, the nayak of Mudlipada- am jail returned and therefore educated enough. Pious brothers I request with folded hands - don't allow the doctors into the village again. That is why our devta has cursed us. God knows what is happening. Two or three are being stolen away by Yam [the Hindu god of death] everyday" (278).

Later when the leader babu (the project officer) somehow convinced them and let the doctors into the villages the doctor advised, "Listen! Be clean, fly away the mosquitoes and the houseflies. Give the children and the patients cow's boiled milk. Wash the fruits and roots before consuming" (279). The doctor had scarcely finished when Baghbindu thundered with anger and shot an arrow at the doctor who somehow saved his life and ran into the room. Baghbindu thundered, "You rescued your life today. It means your life is yet not complete. How dare you ask us to drink cow's blood? You people drink her milk and starve the calf. Now you ask us to do the same! Our Dogoi (the deity) is already displeased with us and now such prescriptions are sure to lead us to doom" (279).

The doctor had no choice but to curse his fate, "Even if five thousand doctors are killed like this it does not matter to the government since the doctor tribe is not endangered. But the white tigers of Nandankanan,

Bhagnavshesh of Konark, the temple of Puri and the bonda tribe are indispensable" (280).

Towards the end, the novel notes the defeat of the Bonda tribes in their battle, to be heard and to receive justice. These lines sum up the tragedy of the tribal people who are up against the wheels of civilisation in order to be crushed by them. The novelist notes- The way to justice and rights is hard. The defeated semi-literate band of Bonda men despair and have learnt a new lesson:

Defeat can not be accepted by self-determining souls. The hands of young bonda men instead of holding kalam (pen) picked up weapons in the darkness of the night. Not to kill the enemy from the outside but for their self-protection. Weapons do not cause just violence they also bring about peace. If weapons cause death they also save lives, this is the hard lesson learnt by the bonds and they try to solve their problems by their own methods which makes sense to them (490)

Adibhhomi depicts how the process of development, progress and assimilation of the tribals into the mainstream society is carried out by the government agencies. The novel exposes the wide gulf that exists between the two forces, the primitive bonda population, on the one hand, and the agencies of the nation-state on the other. The results of enforced 'development' of very different people, without attempting to understand their real nature, aspiration and subjectivity, are doomed from the very start. The modern governments, for various reasons, feel obliged to 'civilise' the so-called 'backward'. The novel showcases what happens when such schemes are carried forward without acquiring a genuine understanding of the beneficiaries.

II

Discussing the theme of exploitation and the subsequent resistance narrated in the novels, it is Yajnaseni by Pratibha Ray that gives an insight into this imperial exploitation of the forest tribes in the time of the Mahabharata which were dominated by the powers in Hastinapur. Yajnaseni, as the novel indicates is primarily a novel with Draupadi as the central character. This novel is a reconstruction of the Mahabharata and it offers a feminine perspective of one of the most maligned female characters of the epic, Draupadi. In addition to Draupadi, the novel also offers a fairer treatment to the contemporary tribal population.

During their exile in the forest, the Pandavas are not sure how the Kirats will receive them. They do settle down, however, not without some resistance.

In comparison to earlier epic texts, this award-winning novel by Pratibha Ray takes a more liberal and compassionate view of the relation between the tribal and the non-tribal population in the day of the Mahabharata. It begins with the misunderstanding and hostility that is generally associated with the tribals' relations with mainstream society. The Pandavas are discusssing the issue of Eklavya. Towards the end of Sahdev's explanation:

To protect the Kurus, Drona, on the pretext of asking for the guru's fee, cruelly asked for the right thumb of his simple, devoted, single-minded disciple, Ekalavaya. How will the kirats forgive that insult by the Kurus and that fee demanded by Drona? That is why they are bent upon destroying the Aryans root and branch (263).

This reflects the suspicion that the tribals and the mainstream society have for each other. Bhim replies, "But Yudhishthir and Arjun had pleaded in favour of accepting tribal Ekalavya as a disciple. Every man is equal" (263). The modern fiction writers' object is to focus on the need to accept this equality of 'everyman' inclusive of the tribal people, In a way this is a reiteration of the contemporary writers' awareness of their responsibility in the postcolonial era as a signifier of their past pitfalls in terms of the atrocities committed towards the tribal population.

The relation between the imperial Hastinapur and its poor tribal pockets around it was necessarily the one of dominance and exploitation of the latter by the former. Example of Eklavya could be the only one of its kind but it indeed symbolizes the relation between the two. Dronacharya may actually have been proud of his tribal disciple who not only worshipped him as his mentor despite having been refused by him to be his disciple since he was not of royal blood, but was also probably one of the most accomplished in the art of archery. He was certainly no less talented than Arjuna if not more. But since Drona could not afford to annoy the royal establishment at Hastinapur, he asked Ekalavya for his right thumb which rendered him incapable of using his skill in warfare to the full.

The kirats understood it all too easily and in retaliation vowed to eliminate those who represented not just Dronacharya but also the royal establishment at Hastinapur. Pandavas had to face this hatred of the Kirats who were genuinely annoyed at the injustice meted out to them. It was only after a series of initial misunderstanding and even fights that the issue was sorted out. It was Draupadi who plays the central role in not only resolving the differences but also in integrating them all. She says:

In Kamyak there will be no distinction of class, caste and race. The injustice inflicted on Ekalavya will have to be made up here. There is enough cause for the Kirats to be annoyed with the Aryans, but by binding them in chains of friendship we will have to bring about the great union of Aryans and non-Aryans (264).

It is Draupadi who takes the initiative in redressing the issues of the past and undoing the atrocities that her dominant community had wrecked upon the vulnerable tribal people.

Meanwhile, Kimir threatens Pandavas. Bhim goes out to fight him. While Bhim is dealing one blow after another, Draupadi intervenes and saves Kimir from imminent death. Then Yudhishthir gave a long speech on how all men and women are equal. He elaborated how in the beginning, for the security of the society and the development of civilization families adopted different occupations which later developed or degenerated into castes. He also pledged friendship with the shabars.

Pratibha Ray describes in detail how the friendship grows between the Pandavas and the Shabars. Both come closer to each other due to two reasons, none had any choice as they had to live side by side in one place. Also, both had limited resources, and hatred and enmity would have done avoidable damage to both. Also, they shared a common enemy, i.e., the Kauravas.

Their friendship is in progress and they eat together in the same place. Draupadi also breastfeeds two of the children who had lost mother in infancy. The friendship goes on and the Shabars also pledge their lifelong friendship with the princes in exile.

Yajnaseni gives a refreshing 'idealistic' view of the otherwise strained relationship of the tribal and the civilised' world. The two worlds have existed alongside each other without communicating effectively. Draupadi therefore, stresses the need to communicate with the Shabars so that the society that considers itself civilised and the other as inferior and savage can understand each other and shun disturbance and suspicion that has continued to dominate and characterise their relationship with one another.

Why *Yajnaseni* breaks new ground is because it 'accepts' that the tribal people have been wronged and that the issue will have to be addressed in a just manner. Also, they recognise why the tribal people are justified in the opposition to the mainstream politics. In fact, the Pandvas even join them in their resistance against the powerful regime of Hastinapur.

Karna - The Rashmirathi of Mahabharata, the Subaltern Kshatriya?

You hold your head high, citing your high-caste
But your comfort is derived from irreligious
exploitation
You tremble with the fear of the brave tribals
Hence you cheat them by asking for the thumb
     (Karna in Ramdhari Singh Dinkar's *Rashmirathi)*

From all accounts of the Mahabharata's Karna's life, one aspect of his life is abundantly clear that his life was governed by two factors, from the beginning to the end: curse (following his birth and the commonly believed lineage), and the remarkable audacity he exhibited in overpowering it. All through his eventful life, Karna had to battle many situations, most pernicious of which was the attitude of the society towards him once they learnt of his less than humble lineage. Not only was he not a kshatriya but he was a soot-putra, the son of a charioteer, a section of the society that was at the very bottom of the Aryan social structure.

The theme of Karna's life is philosophised by Irawati Karve, generalising the predicament of his life and still pointing out the individuality of the suffering. She writes, "Unfulfillment, the Mahabharata tells us again and again, is the normal condition of man... To some extent each major figure in the Mahabharata is defeated by life, but none so completely as Karna" (123). She draws a comparison between his life and that of Vidura, who had the same father as Pandu and Dhritarashtra but could not claim the throne since his mother was a dasi, despite being superior to both his half brothers, mentally and physically.

Karna's story, and to an extent that of Vidura, is a classic study in terms of the situation of the subaltern. He could never shed the burden of his 'subalternity' despite achieving much in life. The denial of equal opportunity even to compete made him bitter to the core. Karve writes, "Karna's defeat lay in just this one fact that he did not know who he was by birth, and when the answer was given to hom, it was too late (124).

Born of the virgin mother Kunti and the Sun god Surya under the effect of the mantra given to her as a boon by rishi Durvasa, Karna was named after the golden ear rings (kundal) that he was born with. Also, he was fabled to have been born through Kunti's ear. Since she could not bear the stigma of being an unwed mother, she placed him in a basket and set it afloat in the Ganges. He was found by the royal charioteer Adhiratha and his wife Radha, much to their pleasure since the couple was childless.

Shivaji Sawant's Mrityunjaya (1967) is a narration by Karan of his lifespan and the events that marked it. It opens with Karna's soliloquy:

There is something I want to say today. It might shock some to hear the dead speaking. But there

Life of Karna, apart from its role in the epic Mahabharata is indeed a commentary on the role of lineage in the Aryan society and the politics involved in it As a young precocious child, Karan desired to be trained by Dronacharya in warfare, which was denied by the royal guru on the ground that he was not of a royal or kshatriya lineage. A dejected Karna then taught himself to be a warrior by considering Surya to be his guru. He would listen about the technique of archery and general warfare and then practice them in the dark. It was only later when he wanted to learn about the divine weapons that he approached Lord Parshuram who only trained Brahmins. Karna lied to him and was thus trained till he reached a point when he equailed his guru. On finding out that he was a kshatriya, Parshuram cursed him so that the most effective of his weapons would delude him when he needed them the most.

It is ironical that Drona refused to accept him as a disciple since he was not a kshatriya and Parshuram cursed him in a rage precisely because he was one. Karna wanted the world to acknowledge that a man of valour should be tested on the merit of his accomplishment and not the virtue of his birth and parentage. It is unfortunate that the prevalent belief of his low birth should have played such role in his destiny and he "...died without finding an answer to what he was and what his rights were" (Karve 140).

There are three important arenas in the life of Karna that clearly define his destiny. These are the arenas that were most deserved by him to be victorious but which, repeatedly due to his lineage, he had to face humiliation and quit, all on the account of his 'low' birth.

The first was the arena that had been organized by the royal guru Dronacharya to showcase the learning of his princes; Kauravas and Pandavas and also announce the most accomplished of them all. Till Karna entered the arena, Arjun was close to being declared the victorious warrior. After Karna's participation the equations changed. Having outshined Arjun in many spheres, Karna challenged him to a duel that would establish the truth about the greatest warrior in all of Aryavrata. It was at that time that Kripacharya intervened and emphasised on the convention of the duel wherein it could only be contested by 'equals', ie, born of the same lincage. It was at that time that Duryodhana realized the potential of the young warrior and coronated him to the throne of Ang (present day Bhagalpur). Despite being the king now, Karna still did not 'qualify' to contest a duel against Arjun. This led to the lifelong enmity between the two and only ended with the death of Karna at the hands of Arjun on the seventeenth day of the war.

It was Duryodhana who, may be for his own interest, takes a leap ahead of the times they were living in as he tries to convince the gathering that a brave man's lineage should not hinder his achievements. It was Duryodhana who thundered towards Bheem, "Valour is the hall-mark of a kshatriya- nor is there much sense in tracing great heroes and mighty rivers to their sources. I could give you hundreds of instances of great men of humble birth- and I know awkward questions might be asked of your own origin. Look at this warrior, his godlike form and bearing, his armour and earrings, and his skill with weapons. Surely there is some mystery about him, for how could a tiger be born of an antelope? Unworthy of being king of Anga, didst thou say? I verily hold him worthy to rule the whole world" (Rajagopalachari 46). Such was his bitterness against the odds presented to him by his fate that he tried to overcome it with not just valour but even arrogance. During the great battle when Duryodhana suspected Bhishma of going soft on the Pandavas, it was Karna who reassurd him, "You can consider the Pandavas dead if Bhishma withdraws from the battle" (Uberoi 322),

The second occasion was the swayamvar of Draupadi. When most of the princes had failed to pierce the eye of the fish, it was Karna who appeared to shoot the arrow, as Angaraj, the king of the state of Ang. As he aimed at the target, it was Draupadi who objected, "You are not a kshatriya. I shall not accept to be a wife or a daughter-in-law of a saarthi (charioteer). I am a kshatriya girl and not a shudra soot-kanya" (Mrityunjay 268).

Karna carried the echo of Draupadi's words for the rest of his life. In fact, after she had uttered her objection, many claimed openly that Kama was a bastard since Adhirath and Radha too were not his real parents. He could not get himself to forgive Draupadi for those remarks and it is ironical that despite being the king of a state he could not yet wash of the 'stigma' of his low birth, though Karna, to the last day of his life remained proud of his parents. Draupadi, in a way, initiated a strained relationship with Karna, and with Arjun finally emerging victorious in the swayamvar, it was turned into hostility and the enmity with Arjun was further deepened since Arjun had 'defeated' him a second time by denial of an equal opportunity to Karna.

Shivaji Sawant and Pratibha Ray differ in their fictional voices or representation as far as the contrasting roles of Draupadi and Karna are concerned. Pratibha Ray's Yajnaseni (1995), the narration of Draupadi of her life in her own words, portrays a different point of view. Since it is the story of Panchali, it depicts her brother Drishtadyumna announcing, "The rules of the contest were made clear at the very beginning. Unless the suitor is high-born, my sister can not wed him However great a hero Karna, the son of a charioteer Adhiratha and Radha, might be, he can not have the right to win my sister" (Yajnaseni, 42). It was this incident that Ray's Yajnaseni recalls as, "This picture of crest fallen Karna filled my heart with compassion and sympathy. Silently I said to myself, "Heroic Karna, if I have the slightest role in the insult and abuse your have suffered, please forgive me. I feel your anguish with all my heart and soul. After this it is my turn to he insulted and shamed. Is it a petty insult for the bride-to-be Krishnaa there should be no bride groom in this world" (43)?

Karan and Draupadi wrestled with their destinies thereafter. Ray emphasizes on the role of this failure in the life of Karna as Rituvati (Karna's first wife) once says to Draupadi, "I am Karna's wife but you are the source of his inspiration. The journey that he is beginning today with the inflexible vow to prove his prowess has become possible only because of you. Had his manhood not been wounded that day in the swayamvar hall, he would not have taken such a vow. You are the supreme failure of his life. Should Karna's life be crowned with any success, that too will be because of you" (184).

On hearing such words from Rituvati, Draupadi laments, "I became absent- minded. For the first time my heart was accepting that injustice had been done to Karna. Man has no control over his birth, but over his acts he does have control. What could be more unjust than that on account of the cursed history of his birth, Kunti's dharma-son, Karna, should be deprived of justice at every step of life" (184).

Whereas Yajnaseni explodes into an angry outburst on the occasion of cheerharan of Draupadi, Mrityunjay contrarily depicts a reaction that was flared up with anger and revenge but doused by constraint. For once Karna felt that Draupadi should now realize that she was a dasi and that now fate had taken her to level that was lower than that of a soot putra. But later when Karna felt the impulse of intervening, he was once more apprehensive and thought that Draupadi might protest and refuse to be protected by a low born soot putra.

A comparative study of the tow texts establishes the contemporary Bhasa authors' sensitivity in terms of the responsibility of a writer. Both have delineated their protagonists in the light of righteousness. Both have taken care not to betray any sense of feeling of superiority in their protagonists. Where Yajnaseni shows Draupadi's expression of sympathy for Karna and shifts the burden of humiliating Karna on her brother, Mrityunjay blames Draupadi for the bitter remarks against him while absolving him of similar comments towards Draupadi that other texts show as Karna's doing.

Works Cited:

Achebe, Chinua. Things Fall Apart. 1958. New York: Anchor Books, 1994. Print.

Alam, Javeed. "Fragmented Culture and Strangulated Existence: Jharkhand's Cultural Encounter with the Modern". Continuity and Change in Tribal Society. Ed. Mrinal Miri. Shimla : IIAS, 1993. Print.

Bhattacharya, B.K. Marityunjaya, 1998. Trans. K.P.S. Magadh. New Delhi: Bhartiya Jnanpith, 2005. Print.

Damodaran, Vinita. "Indigenous Forests: Rights, Discourses, and Resistance in Chota Nagpur, 1860-2002." Ecological Nationalisms: Nature, Livelihoods, and Identities in South Asia. Ed. Gunnel Cederlof and K. Sivaramakrishnan. New Delhi: Permanent Black, 2005. Print.

Devi, Mahashweta, and Usha Ganguly Rudali: From Fiction to Performance. Trans. Anjum Katyal. Calcutta: Seagull, 1997. Print.

Ferguson, Niall. Empire: How Britain Made the Modern World. 2003. New Delhi: Penguin, 2008. Print.

Ghosh, Kaushik. "A Market for Aboriginality: Primitivism and Race Classification in the Indentured Labour Market of Colonial India" (8-48). Subaltern Studies, 1999. Ed. Gautam Bhadra, Gyan Prakash and Susic Tharu. Vol. X. New Delhi: OUP, 2005. Print.

Guha, Ranajit. "Dominance Without Hegemony and Its Historiography" (210-309). Subaltern Studies. 1989. Ed. Ranajit Guha. New Delhi: OUP, 2005. Print.

Katyal, Anjum, ed. "The Metamorphosis of 'Rudali'" (Introductory essay 1-53). Rudali: From Fiction to Performance. By Mahasweta Devi and Usha Ganguly. Calcutta: Seagull, 1997. Print.

Linkenback, Antje Forest Futures: Global Representations and Ground Realities in the Himalayas Ranikhet: Permanent Black, 2007. Print.

Mankad, Piyush "Seeing Like a State - Why Well-Meaning Development Projects Founder When They Don't Involve End Users in the Process", Indian Express. 08 December 2009. Print.

Mohanty, Gopinath. Matiataal, 1964. Trans. Shankarlal Purohit. New Delhi: Jnanpith, 2001. Print

_ _ _. *Paraja*. 1945. Trans. Bikram K. Das. New Delhi: OUP, 1987. Print.

Nautiyal, Vidyasagar. Searching for Identity Across the Border. Amar Ujaia. Dehrarlun: 08 October, 2007. Print.

New York Times. Wild Tribes of India Becoming Civilized Lord Curzon's Trip Through Remote Districts. December 22, 1901. Google Book Search Web. 30 June 2008.

Rajagopalachari, C. Mahabharata, 1951. New Delhi Bhartiya Vidya Bhavan, 2009. Print.

Ray, Pratibha. Aadibhoomi 1993. Trans. Shankarlal Purohit. New Delhi: Jnanpith, 2001. Print.

_ _ _. *Yajnaseni*. 1995. Trans. Pradip Bhattacharya. New Delhi: Rupa, 2002. Print.

Reddy, Vijay Raghav. Book Review. Doosra Narak Kund by Jaiwanti Dimri. Chhatisgarh Today. October-December 2004. Print.

Sagreiya, K. P. Forests and Forestry. 1967. New Delhi: National Book Trust, 1994. Print.

Sawant, Shivaji. Mrityunjay. 1974. Trans. Om Shivaraj, New Delhi: Jnanpith, 2000. Print.

Spivak, Gayatri Chakravorty, trans. Foreword. Choti Munda and His Arrow. 1980. By Mahasweta Devi. Calcutta: Seagull, 2002. Print.

Uberoi, Meera. The Mahabharata. 1996, New Delhi: Penguin, 2005. Print.

Chapter - 4

Bad History, Worse Logic? The Politics of Godhood

The Rationale of Ulgulan

My shoulders bleed of begaar
Zamindar's sepoy rebukes me day and night
I weep all the time
This is what begaar has done to me
Homeless am 1, who will comfort me?
Weeping day and night
My blood has turned saline.

(Aranyer Adhikar 33)

The greatest contribution of Mahashweta Devi in writing the novel *Aranyer Adhikar* has been the manner in which she has been able to portray the life and times of one of the greatest and most inspiring icons of pre-independent India. She provided the much needed fictional space to the process of 'decolonising imagination of urban India' (Roycroft 67) and brought alive the character of a revolutionary who had been trashed in the official reports of the Raj, sympathised with in Sarat Chander Roy's The Mundas and their Country (1912) and worshipped in the folklore of Chotanagpur While the British government was terrified of Ulgulan (the uprising led by Birsa Munda) and, therefore, rubbished Birsa's claim to heroism; Roy

"...saw missionaries as acknowledged authorities on tribal India" (57). It was with the publication of K S Singh's Birsa Munda and His Movement (1966) that a balanced portrayal of the tribal hero, based on folk lores, missionary and offical archives, was given.

Historiography, as far as involving the tribals is concerned, had repeatedly been marred, as Asad established"...general connection between anthropological knowledge and the expansion of European power" (Patricia Uberoi et al 13). Similarly, Edward Said (1979) and Bernard Cohn (1990) have both pointed to the manner in which orientalist or anthropological 'knowledge' of a country's traditions and customs helped to fix sociological categories, such as caste, ritual, law, and political institutions, into a timeless essence that denied the necessity for administrators to concern themselves with the changing political aspirations and concerns of people living on the ground.

Anthropological projects carried out under the patronage of the colonial government made intervention by the government look almost necessary. After studying the tribes of Chotanagpur, one of the leading anthropologists of pre-independent India, Sarat Chandra Roy (1912 and 1915) advocated a larger role for the administration. Quoting from Roy's The Oraons of Chotanagpur (1915), Sangeeta Dasgupta writes:

He believed that under British guidance the 'primitive tribes" of Chotanagpur would eventually chart their journcy towards progress. "Providence in His mercy, had brought the mighty British Lion to

*introduce law and order into the distracted country'
of Chotanagpur" (ibid. 31). "These young brethren
of humanity, so long lagging behind in the race of
life, are being at length launched on the forward
path of social, intelluctual, moral and material
progress" (ibid. 248). Their "...upliftment... would
be one of the noblest of the innumerable noble
achievements of the British Government in India in
the cause of humanity and civilization" (ibid. 123)
In other words, a tribal community lacked self-
generating tendencies and required the aid of
external agencies to give it momentum (Dasgupta
149).*

The main focus of the rebellions in the tribal
heartland revolved around the single demand of
restoration of land rights to 'first settlers' that they
claimed themselves to be. They claim to be the absolute
masters of their soil, forests and ultimately their
destinies. All these demands converged into their
liberation from the dikku. They romanticized their past
where access to forests and agricultural land was
uninhibited. Dhani Munda often talked to Bharmi
Munda in the jail about the first settlement of their
ancestors in the place that was later known as
Chotanagpur. Old Dhani Munda would relate with
nostalgia, "Many many years ago the forefather of the
forefathers of Birsa, probably even their forefathers,
searched around for land in order to settle. In those days
the hills, the jungle and the fields were free of
anybody's ownership. They were two brothers, Chutya
Haram and Nagu. It was after the names of those two

that the entire area came to be known as Chotanagpur" (Aranyak Adhikar 30).

The entire history of the Mundas (and other tribes) was thus based on folk memories and, of course, lacked written documents. Also, with the passage of time they lagged behind in terms of sophistication and power to cambat any gradual and atic encroachment on their rights over the resources. Of the 79,714 square systematic kilometres area of Chotanagpur- Santhal Pargana plateau, more than 33 percent was covered by dense forest (Sarkar 97). The present day tribals are widely understood to have been the first inhabitants of the land. The villages of the original settlers were known as Kunti-katti hatus (villages) literally meaning those who cut the first post. The chief characteristics of the then tribal society were a subsistence level barter economy where everyone had equal rights and no one owned any property privately. All the members held joint possession of natural resources such as agricultural land and forests. It was an egalitarian society where no one ruled anyone. The Mundas and the Uraons had slowly evolved Parhas or confederacies of several villages, each for the settlement of inter-village disputes and the regulation of the customary tribal laws.

About the sixth century AD the Mundas and the Uraons jointly selected a common leader or raja (Ekka 396) who was probably known by the name of Phani Mukut Rai, the first of the Nagbansi kings (Sarkar 98). His position was not that of a king in the regular sense but only of a leader in case of defence against an external aggression. He was provided voluntary contribution in kind and a few days of free labour in a year. A descendant of this leader was made a tributary of the Moghuls in the year 1585. One of the descendants, probably the 42nd Nagbansi king Durjan Sal was taken prisoner by the Moghuls for defaulting on payments of arrears. Thus the Nagbansi king was reduced to tribute paying jagirdar to the Moghul Governor of Bihar. It was during this phase of tribal history that the traditional Khunt-katti village system was gradually transforming into jagirdari system (landlordism) and the Khunt-kuttidars were gradually subjected to feudal exploitation. Despite introducing a somewhat forced land revenue system, the Moghul administration did not interfere directly with the way of life and modes of production of the tribal economy. They continued to enjoy unrestricted movement into the forest areas and the utilisation of its land and produce.

It was only with the advent of British empire that the real trouble began for the tribals. It was around 1765 when British administration began in Chotanagpur. Most of the tribal belt of Bihar was brought under direct control of the alien government in 1793. With the establishment of courts and the police station in the Chotanagpur area in 1832, British administration made its presence felt in concrete terms. Christian missionaries followed in 1845

Birsa Munda's rebellion does not come into existence in a vaccum, and if one takes an overall view of agrarian/ peasant revolt across India, it is a fitting sequel to what preceded it and is an inspiration to those who followed him. From the Paharia revolt of 1772 to the 1922 full scale guerilla war of Alluri Ramachandra

Raju there have been revolts in various parts of the country and Birsa'a Ulgulan falls rightly between the first war of Indian Independence of 1857 and the Satyagraha of the 1920s. What is common in these uprisings is the target of collective anger - the Establishment; on most occasions the imperial British government. The background to these uprisingss is socio-economic, which, if stripped to its core element has only one characteristic - agrarian.

Coming to the Chotanagpur areas the battlefield of Birsa's calling- the root cause of public anguish was the appropriation of the rights of the tribal population over the use of forests and proprietorship of agricultural land. By the beginning of the nineteenth century the British government opened the tribal belts of Chotanagpur, (in line with their practice elsewhere) to the enterprising thikadars (contractors) from the plains who could put the agricultural land to more productive use and thus fetch more revenue for the government. According to an estimate there were more than 600 jagirdars in Chotanagpur by 1856. The rising power of the Jagirdars was possible only at the cost of the receding proprietorship of the tribals over their land. Since tribals did not have the custom of private ownership of land or any resources, the written records of land and its ownership were thus absent. The absence of written language and documents all over the tribal world made matters worse.

The so called civilised world used its 'written' culture to the optimum as Ajay Skarna notes, "The notion of writing as a weapon of the dominant is thus often a crucial element in the experience of subaltern groups" (14). This made the confiscation /purchase of tribal lands much simpler than in other parts of the country. By 1874 Mundas' authority over their own land was almost over and the entire Munda population had been reduced to labourers on their own land, working round the year to just help produce enough to feed their family and pay interest on their loans, the balance of which incresed after each year anyway.

K S Singh, however, believes that the attitude of the rebels was naïve and that the myth under-lying the slogan 'all lands to the tribals', has survived with an extra- ordinary pertinacity in the region (Singh 1972: 349). The root of this myth could be found in the ideas of the Sardars, which were shaped by their folk memory and the education they had received in the mission schools. He quotes Haldar and insists the original tribal order was described as one of Arcadian simplicity:

The Kols, Mundaries and Uraons are the aboriginals of the district. In the ancients times they had no kings and no chiefs and were divided into families, and kept together by their "parhas" or Conferences. The fields they had cleared and prepared were their own, yet the whole belonged to them. After a time a part of the Uraons and Mundaries in the new so-called Bhooinhar patti of Chotanagpur chose a king and for his maintenance gave him a grant in land, viz., half of the fields of each village. The other half the Kols - kept for themselves as their own and this they retained possession without any rent for it till the establishment of the British courts in 1832 (349).

Singh continues, "Such a view of history overlooked the essentially composite character of the society in the exposed tribal region. Under its spell the tribes would demand nothing short of a restoration of the state of things that prevailed before the influx of the "aliens" (349). This was 'bad history and worse logic. It is rightly pointed out that with such rationale, the movement couldn't get much further. With such an idea backing the revolution, it would be necessary to trace the most original inhabitants, and then restore everything to them. The new administrators would then have to be satisfied to play the role of mere mediators in the restoration process. Singh writes further,

> *As regards the renewal of the primitive Arcadian State so much desired by the petitioners it seems to me that it would be quite as reasonable for the British Government to aid the Kols in the fulfilment of their desire as to restore to the Hindus the whole of Hindustan and not only to withdraw their own government but also help the Hindus in driving away the Musalmans from it (350).*

Referring to the historical truths time and again and thus attempting to justify it to oust all the later entrants could at best be described as utopian and even quixotic but the leaders of the rebellions found it most suitable to rally their followers around this point alone. It was the extreme stand upon which they built their strategy. As far as unhindered rights to the forests were concerned, the Imperial government had no intention even to concede that much since the vast forests would provide the colonial enterprise with wealth and resources. Singh further states that,

> *It is historically true that the Aryan Hindus by some means or other had reduced the Kols of Chotanagpur to a state of serfdom. When law and order were introduced into the country by the British Government the Kols began gradually to realise their actual position, the European Christian missionaries came in and took the Kols by hand. The crude tradition of the Mundas and Uraons thus found development by association with men of higher culture into an ideal picture of a happy state of innocence in olden days; and as interchange of thought increased under the fostering influence of internal peace and of struggles going on elsewhere was brought home to the Kols, the idea of their supposed rights attained the highest pitch of extravagance. The Government cannot but leave these ideas alone (350).*

Singh explains that the disastrous failure of the Sardar movement in the 19th century was due to heavy reliance on this myth... [worse] the hang-over persists; it does not still make for a rational and dispassionate consideration of the agrarian issue (351).

The question that arises is: Did Birsa realise, due to his exposure to education and the ways of the sophisticated world, that his struggle needed better history and a still better logic? Or was he too under the spell of the hang-over? Did the Sardars fail because of their 'extravagant ideas' or because they lacked the killing instinct of a Birsa? As the Sardars would later complain to Birsa, "We fought a lot. The total papers used by the Sardars for writing applications to the British Government could be sufficient to cover the entire Chotanagpur plateau. All the ink used is more than the water of a flooded river" (Aranyar Adhikar 176).

Sardars' lamentation over the failure of peaceful and legal efforts echo a similar effort put in by Birsa himself when he 'filed' an application at the Chaubasa forest post, claiming the tribals' land for his community and was laughed at. Ranajit Guha explains, painstakingly, to shatter the myth of the tribal discontentment erupting into violence without much provocation. He elaborates how the Rangpur dhing against Debi Sinha (1783), the Barasat bidroha led by Titu Mir (1831), the Santal hool (1855), the 'blue mutiny' of 1860 and the Munda [uprising] of 1899-1900... where the 'protagonists in cach case had tried out petitions, deputations or other forms of supplications before actually declaring war on their oppressors' (Guha 1983: 2).

Birsa did realise that the battle that he intended to wage was against an enemy who was not only powerful but also many-headed, which worked through the landlord, police, court, and finally, the military. That was probably not enough to deter his ambition or of those tribals who had risen in rebellion against the empire before him. After all he did not aim to defeat the empire in an overall battle for all its territories but just wanted 'outsiders' of all colours and backgrounds to leave his jungle mother alone. That was a battle which he thought was, winnable.

Ever since the tribal belts across India came into direct contact with the mighty empires since the days of the Mahabharata and Ramayana, conflicts and confrontations have been the direct result. Thereafter many tribal territories have had trouble dealing with the outsiders. Throughout history, from Ashoka to the Moghuls, there have been misunderstandings and skirmishes between the tribals pockets and the imperial armies and civilians. Somehow things had always been solved amicably and the tribals always managed to retreat into their domains, without necessarily losing their liberty. The colonial experience was very different as, "...there is evidence to suggest that although the governments that preceded the British, appropriated certain parts of the forests for Imperial purposes, and regulated the cutting of the trees by local residents in other parts, the inhabitants were allowed to obtain all the produce they required for domestic and agricultural purposes from the public forests without hindrance" (Saldanha 70). Till then the State did not view the forests as a revenue generating commercial enterprise. Unlike the agrarian classes in the rest of the country, for the tribal population the forest was not only a source for fuelwood and grazing for their cattle; it also provided them various fruits and roots during the drought period (Fernandes 49). For them it was a habitat:

Among the Mundas of Chotanagpur ara is the generic term for edib le leaves of all vegetables either cultivated or self-sown used them as potherbs. Hoffman (1950: 178-187) mentions 71 different wild plants used by the Mundas as potherbs, 26 of whose tubers, corns and roots are used as vegetables, 15 trees and shrubs where young leaves are used as potherbs, 10 others whose young leaves are eaten raw and of 25 wild trees and plants whose flowers are used as vegetables. The author also enumerates 17 cultivated fubers and roots that are used as food, 28 plants cultivated for other purposes ans used also as potherbs and 14 plants cultivated as potherbs. Even the food habits of a semi-Hinduised tribe like the Saoras of Orissa show their great dependence of the forest (49).

However, with the advent of the British empire situation was totally changed, and, for the worse. It was so for a variety of reasons. This was a modern day empire that was not just disproportionately more powerful but was also equipped with modern methods of governance. Also, this regime had centuries of experience dealing with similar or even much more hostile situations all over the globe from Australia, Africa and Middle east to the Americas. What can be singled out to be the most compelling reasons is that this empire's requirements for the upkeep of its machinery was also monstrous in scale. Tribal world provided it with the abundant natural resources which it found had been inhabited by people who not only wasted it away in devastating agricultural practices such as rab (Saldanha 74) but also had no other use for the nature's bounty. The British needed the timber for the Royal Navy and the network of railways. The imperial government was fully aware of the importance of the wealth of the forests:

The exhaustion of the forests due to over-exploitation appears to have first attracted the attention of the colonial government in 1837. The teak forests of North Konkan provided the much needed timber to the Royal Navy in the early nineteenth century. By this time British merchants were active in teak trade, they included both private firms and also the East India Company officials in their private capacity. Maximization of revenue from forest products, especially teak, dominated the early British interests in forests. That Thana forests were being destroyed at an alarming rate, was evident even by 1840s. This was reported by Dr. Gibson, Superintendant of Forest for Bombay presidency, the colonial Jervis, Chief Engineer at Bombay and member of the Military Board. In 1841, the first prohibitory order was issued which banned the cutting of teak trees in government forests in one taluka of the district. Between 1847 and 1862 several resolutions relating to the rights of the cultivators of trees were introduced (71).

It is unfortunate that when it came to preserving those forests for commercial or ecological purposes, the price had to be paid by the tribals, who it is quite certain, did not exploit the forests for any commercial purposes and treated it as sacred.

Since the beginning of the nineteenth century, the British government had been imposing restrictions of various types in various parts of the country over the locals' use of forests. They began to realise an ever-increasing need for raw material as they consolidated their territorial position in the subcontinent, "It is ironic that the hill tracts formerly written off by British administrators as virtually worthless and merely a source of danger to the adjacent plains, came in the late nineteenth century to be seen as an area of great economic potential and soon had to be open[ed] out for the benefit of the world at large... a vast tract of fertile, inaccessible but potentially productive country, rich in minerals and in other natural assets, sparsely populated and hitherto underdeveloped" (Arnold 107-8). More often than not the ecological reason was given as a pretext under the cover of which commercial exploitation by the regime to enhance its infrastructure continued and at the same time benefitted its entrepreneurs. Most of these restrictions and the anxieties of the government culminated in the Forest Act of 1878 which made the government the supreme owner of the forests and disenfranchised the common citizens; especially the tribais population from unrestricted use of forests (Linkenback 2007.127).

Aranyer Adhikar opens with the news of the death of Birsa Munda on the ninth June 1900 A few lines later the reader is introduced to the greatest irony of the life of Mundas who 'can have rice only in their dreams' (Aranyar Adhikar 9). As Birsa often complained, "Why should Munda eat only ghato? Why can't they have rice llike the Dikoo?" Rice in this case is not just the cereal for food but a symbol of being the owners of your own land, dignity and independence. Mahasweta Devi mentions in the same opening of the novel that 'somehow it is the dream of having rice that controls the destiny of Birsa.' It was rice that finally sealed his destiny too. While he had issued strict instructions to Sali not to light fire, while Birsa slipped into sleep, she began to cook rice for him. It was the smoke that thus rose into the blue sky that led his informers to captuure him. Rice is thus the symbol of their struggle. As mentioned before, the root cause of these rebellions has been the alienation of the aboriginals from their land and natural resources and their subseqrent subjugation.

It is, however, interesting to note that these rebellions rose with the ascendency of the might of the British government. The indigenous agents were of course responseble for direct exploitation of the native dwellers but with the advent of the British power the practice of thikadars in the tribal areas increased and also their exploitative tendencies were on their maximum since they enjoyed protection from the British government. The rajas too no longer feared the tribal rebellion since they could count on the mighty British army to counter any such uprising.

As has been argued in the discussion on Gopinath Mohanty's Paraja, Mahashweta Devi's Rudaali and Pratibha Ray's Aadibhoomi among many others, how the native agents of civilization were instrumental in ruining the unsuspecting and the vulnerable tribal population, These agents were the landlords, who were mostly outside settlers and the government officials,

Ranajit Guha remarks, "Dominance in colonial India was doubly articulated. It stood, on the one hand, for Britain's power to rule over its South Asian subjects, and on the other, for the power exercised by the indigenous elite over the subaltern amongst the subject population itself.... With colonialism, dominance was substantiated by the authority of the state" (69).

Who is the Dikku that the Mundas (like other tribals) detest, fear and, if one might say, even want to be, if they could. Javeed Alam explains that the villagers contrast the Dikku in their linguistic usage in a binary opposition with HOR. The tribal people are HOR. HOR is human, that is, one with attributes which go to define the humaneness. Dikku,, is one who lacks in these attributes. Dikku is a face like ours but one who does not have any of those attributes that make a man human. Dikku is one who represents inhumaneness amongst us. Alam continues "The Dikku can not relate to you as an equal and you therefore cannot relate to him at all, he can never share anything with you, you cannot decide with him about matters social because he is going to turn and deceive you. He divides the social existence of the people wherever he steps in. He only covets the possessions of others including the human body in its female form" (10-11).

The direct result of this confrontation of the Dikku and the tribal people was not the subjugation of the tribal population in the long run but also the change of character of the latter. That is not to say that tribals did not show any inclination towards vice but what can be stressed upon is the fact that the tribals became more offensive and retaliatory with the passage of time and mounting atrocities. Aranyer Adhikar mentions an incident of 1895 when hundreds of Mundas walked for miles overnight to witness the trial of Birsa, that is, when he was first held captive, tried publicly and sentenced to two years in prison. The native policeman explains to Colonel Gordon that the Mundas were simply marching to see the trial of the one they considered God and that he could assure him that they would not inflict any damage on anyone. He continues, "Earlier they used to attend our festivals. But now these zamindars such as Jagmohan Singh and Suraj Singh have turned them violent by subjecting them to bonded labour, digging their fields and by having their crops run over by elephants on the pretext of non-payment of interest on the loaned money"(Aranyar Adhikar 124).

Apart from the Biblical references to the night of Birsa's birth there is nothing to hint anything extraordinary about Birsa in his early years. It is believed that on the night of his birth three stars were seen in the sky. That strenghtened the belief that Birsa was a divine incarnation, much to the sorrow of his mother who always feared that she would have to part with him one day. Before Birsa's birth his parents had to leave Sugana's paternal village of Ulihatu following a dispute. The family wandered in search of livelihood, while a son Komta, and two daughters Daskir and Champa were born. When they settled down in Bamba for a while, Birsa was born on a Thursday. Following his birth they migrated to Chalkad, Sugana's mother's village. Before coming to Chalkad the entire family converted to Christianity at a German mission.

Birsa grew up in Chalkad while spending almost all his time in the forests. He had an almost miraculous affinity with the forests and its ways. The fables of his mastery over the paths, tough terrain and various animals, herbs and fruits in the forests spread all over the region. It was strange how the nature mother opened up her treasures to him. This led Sugana and Karmi to warn Birsa time and again to 'be like others' and prompted his father to look for a suitable employment for his son in the field of some zamindar as befits any Munda boy his age. Meanwhile Birsa's younger brother Kanu was born. With the passage of time Sugana found himself under debt of fourteen to fifteen rupees on account of his two daughters' weddings. Providing for his family was proving to be a difficult task. Komta was therefore sent to Kundi Bartoli to work for Bhura Munda. Birsa was sent to Karmi's father Diboi Munda's house at Ayubhatu where Karmi's sister Joni looked after her sister's son with great care. It was at his relatively prosperous maternal grandfather's house that Birsa discovered that there is more to eat than just the ghato that he and his family had eaten all their life.

Birsa and his brother Komta grew up with the dream of providing their mother 'a sackful of salt' so that she could add that to the ghate as they knew that they seldom got to eat ghato with salt and that their mother deprived herself of even that luxury and hence was growing weak.

Joni smiled and said, "You will stay with us Birsa. Why will you go to another land?"

Birsa, "I have promised my mother. I am a grown up man now."

"What will you do by growing up?"

"I will get a sackful of salt for my mother, and dal and grains." (50)

Birsa was sent to the school of Jaipal Nag at Salga. He made a remarkable progress at school. At home Joni gave him a variety of vegetables, meat and grains to eat. After some time when Joni got married, Birsa joined her and went to her new house at Khatanga. He too had wanted to move out of that place having learnt a few things at school, he now realised that his destination lay elsewhere. He also worried who would feed him if he didn't go with Joni. Since people at Ayabhatu had grown fond of Birsa, they pleaded with him not to leave them. His maternal aunt pleaded, "Ayubhatu will be deserted Birsa. Who will play the flute for us and who will dance playing *tuila*?"

Jaipal Nag pleaded, "Don't go Birsa. There is no one like you at school. I will teach you whatever I know." His playmates pleaded, "Don't go Birsa. Akhara will be deserted"(52).

Birsa only replied, "I have to be a big man. Will that be possible here?" (53)

That was a formative period of Birsa's life. He wanted to break free but from what and how, he did not know. He was unaware of the vibrations emanating from the surroundings, from within and from the jungle. Mahashweta Devi observes:

Birsa did not know, Joni did not know, Jaipal Nag did not know and Birsa's playmates did not know what outside attraction was pulling him from outside the Mundari world and from outside life? Overwhelming, indomitable attraction. Mundari life crushed under a thousand restrictions and numerous beliefs. Today you are Mundari, tomorrow a christian, then Munda, again christian, but today you are named Sugana, Komta, Dolka, Bharmi, Dhani; tomorrow Daud, Mathew, Johana, Abraham- no matter what, always present in blood will be the reign of Simboda, that of Haram Asool (53).

Herein lay the seeds of rebellion. It was the desire to break free from the clutches of destiny, even if that meant breaking away from the shackles of being a Munda. Mahasweta traces the developments in the character of Birsa from that early age. She demonstrates the early traits of his rebellion in his desire to be a big man. And he knew that he can not achieve that by being in Ayubhatu. He was ready to try his hands at various things. He wanted to attempt many things, knowing very well that as a Munda his destiny was somewhat sealed but he was preparing for a showdown with his own destiny.

Birsa's destiny was part of a socio-historical 'truth' that had been driven into his psyche, like any other Munda, that when Simboda annihilated the demons, their wives pleaded before him- and Simboda caught hold of them by their hair and flung the minto the deep jungles. It was since that time that their evil spirits haunt the jungles and fields. It was also widely believed that the fury of those evil spirits was more powerful than that of all men and women. Those spirits, in their various disguised form, misled the Munda men and women and them murdered them in the deep forests. Birsa wasn't untouched by these beliefs of his fellowmen,

Birsa grew up with these beliefs. He knows how millions of Mundas lead their lives once they are born as Mundas, and he is aware of the blasphemy of contemplating any other way of life now that he is born a Munda But Birsa is preparing to commit that very sin. It was no more in his control to douse the spark of rebellion that was beginning to ignite in his blood (53).

With a desire to leave for a new place in order to give his life a new chance and also haunted by the worry of who would feed him in Ayabhatu in the absence of Joni, Birsa accompanied her to her husband's village in Khatanga where Joni kept him like her son. He lived there happily except that Joni's husband stopped his schooling saying, "I can not stand an educated Munda. Take cows for grazing, eat to your fill and dance in the akhara. When a Munda becomes educated, he dies like a dikku" (54).

Birsa couldn't go against Joni's husband, his mausa, because he was highly feared and respected for his great knowledge of cures of various ailments and above all, witchcraft. Therefore he tolerated his decisions and carried out the chores entrusted to him with devotion because the mausa, otherwise did not interfere in any aspects of his life and was even fond of him. It was there that Birsa realised that he was beginning to understand what led to human weakness. He understood that getting enough to eat and wear also makes people weak in its own manner. The two people he thought about were his father and Joni. His father Sugana grew weak and docile because he never had enough to eat and feed his family and therefore did not want to offend anyone in any manner. Joni, on the other hand grew subjugated and weak for the fear of offending anyone by her free will, her husband in particular, for the fear of losing the comforts of her life. It is this weakness, arising invariably out of availablity or the absence of comforts in life, that frightened Birsa and which he wanted to overcome.

Joni wanted him to stay with her in her house and learn all about medicines and witchcraft from her husband. Birsa could have reasoned it out with her, refering to what he had learnt at the mission. He could have said what they say at the mission, "Nasan Bonda, Nag are fictitious. Simbonda Haram Asool is false. Most of the diseases, such as cholera are spread through stagnant water" (56).

Next stage of Birsa's life began in the German mission at Burju. That is when he ran away from Joni's house, having being beaten by her husband after he committed negligence of duty and the cattle ruined Ghasi Munda's crops Later Birsa understood that his destiny was dragging him out of the Mundari world. Birsa considered it a moment of emancipation from the shackles of belonging that had glued him to his past for far too long. At the German mission Reverend Puttsking found him a boy of promise. He passed lower primary in two years. It was then that the Reverend advised him to continue his studies at Chaibasa since he felt his future was bright.

At home Sugana tried to convince his son to begin working in the garden of the sahib of the mission since he will be able to live a happy life and get plenty of rice to eat as the gardener of the sahib. Seeing a resolute Birsa, Sugana continued, "What will you gain by studying further? You will only become more restless. You will look down upon the other Mundas and still nobody will call you a babu. Nobody will make you the mukhiya of your village. Then you will end up as a coolie in a coal mine or a tea estate" (57). It was only when Birsa told him, "After education I will become like the sahib, sahib himself assured me" that Sugana finally conceded. Birsa was indeed encouraged by his achievements at the primary school. He wanted to study and be like the sahibs.

It was at the Chaibasa mission school that Birsa met Amulya, an orphan who could speak Mundari despite being a Bengali. Birsa was able to strike a semblance of friendship with Amulya on the very first day at the school. Birsa asks him on the first day, "Will you become a dikku when you grow up, just like other babus?"

"Others might be. I won't."
"What will you become?"
"Doctor. I will be in government service."
"Then you will be a dikku." (68)

Birsa carried with him his distrust of the dikku wherever he went. He shared his community's belief that whosoever is educated enough and in government service must necessarily be a dikku. He had his own plan for himself which included 'learning a lot and to go to court to reclaim my father's land' (68). His plan did not end with the reclamation of his father's land from the 'aliens' but also to be a preacher and spread the name of Christ.

While at the mission school, Birsa came into contact with several sardars involved in the mulkai ladai (the battle for the motherland). It was when Father Nottrett called the sardars - thugs, Birsa was finally disenchanted with the Christian missionaries. He rebelled against the missionary and followed in line with that of the sardars who too had been Christians but were disenchanted with it and now fulfilling the promise of the mulkai ladai. It was then that Birsa realised the fact of sab sahib ek topi, that all the sahibs belonged to the same category and were interested in keeping the munda people in the illusion of the kingdom of heaven. Birsa let his fellows realise that the Munda had no place in the kingdom of heaven and for them the real kingdom was their own kingdom, ie, the kingdom of Chotanagpur.

Mahashweta Devi traces the evolution of Birsa into Dharti Aba step by step and, through her powerful imagination gives a realistic account of the various early stages of his life. After breaking away from the missionary, Birsa left for Bandgaon to Anand Pandey who was the munshi of zamindar Jagmohan Singh. This was a new beginning for Birsa in the Vaishnavite ashram. It was here that he wore the sacred thread and studied the holy Hindu scriptures. He worshipped Tulsi plant (basil) and also travelled around the villages with his teacher. Anand Pandey and his brother Sukhnath noticed the rostlessness in Birsa and said:

"Be at peace Birsa. Worship and recite His name on the Tulsi rosary."
"That may bless you people with peace, will it grant the same to Mundas?"
"To one and all Birsa."
"Our god is different. We are the subjects of Sing Bonga."
"God is one Birsa, Krishna Bhagwan" (80).

Birsa would go to the forests and the play on his flute by the pond in the evenings. This was the time when two tribal girls Gunja and Rata offered themselves in marriage to Birsa, a proposal he declined without any second thought. One day he was contacted by Bharmi. Daso and Matari, who had been sent by his father to inform him of the implementation of the Forest Act of 1878, which disenfranchised the tribal population from the right to the unrestricted use of the forests. This marked the beginning of his struggle with the administration.

They went to the forest post in Chaibasa and filed an application claiming the right to the forest, much to the amusement of the officials there who only ridiculed the attempt saying, "Swim across the oceans to the

Queen. She trembles at the mention of the Mundas"(83).

On returning to Bandgaon, Birsa learnt that he was no longer acceptable at Pandey's ashram for siding with the sardars which would incur the displeasure of the zamindars.

"Had I not been a Munda would you have still turned me away? Now that the Mundas claim their rights, that's why you turn them away."

"Go away Birsa and worship your Sing Bonga."

"I won't worship Sing Bonga, not your Thakur either" (84),

Birsa returned home and finding nothing to eat went into the forest and exhumed the recently buried body of Chalki Mundani to take out the silver ring and a few coins that he was sure she would not need in heaven. With this he bought rice in the Satruday haat but before that the news had been spread throughout Chalkad by his brother Komta's brother in law. His mother flung the rice away which infuriated Birsa and he retreated into the forests.

Caught between the need for survival of an unorganised and unsophisticated people and the commercial greed of an ever-expanding political empire, Birsa and his 'fellow' rebels, over the centuries, fought a lonesome battle. They fought it, unaware of each other's mutual anxieties, in little battlefields of their own against the pan- Indian presence of a regime which had little trouble in concentrating its energies in those areas from time to time in order to crush any such 'disturbances' in numerous areas inhabited by numerous people in its vast empire on which the sun never set. At the core of Birsa's Ulgulan was the forest. 'The fire of Ulgulan does not ravish the forest. It burns the heart and blood of man. That fire does not burn the jungle. For the Mundas, jungle rujuvenates itself like a mother- like Birsa's mother, the children of the jungle sit in its lap'(10). It was the forest, that embraced its (aboriginal) children, and for those children the world beyond those forest was always mysterious. It provided them plenty during the harvest, provided them in abundance the varous varieties of its splendid wealth and sustained the entire population during the lean periods of pre-harvest months and drought.

That is why Birsa had claimed the right to the forest. His Ulgulan was founded on bold proclamation - "He shall liberate the forest from the clutches of the dikoo. Jungle was the mother of the Mundas and the dikoo had demeaned her. Birsa intended to purify her through the fire of the Ulgulan. Thus followed the claim of the Mundas and Ho, Kols, Santhals and Uraons to the ownership of the forests, right to the forests of Chota Nagpur and the right of ownership to the forests of Palamu, Singhbhoomi and Chakradharpur- so that they could dwell in the lap of their mother" (10).

Birsa returned a few days later as Bhagwan, the news of which preceded his arrival at Chalkad and he finally announced to his mother, "My people wanted a Bhagwan, mother. I have returned as one" (92).

The Politics of Godhood

The role of rumour

Somewhere between the extremely polarised viewpoints of Birsa as this young monkey' who was 'fraud' and claimed to be God's 'incarnation', the one held by the missionaries (Roycroft 60); and the one believed by the Mundas as Bhagwan who would liberate them from the 'Kingdom of the Demon' (the British Raj), Mahasweta Devi presents the real Birsa; a man who was a true revolutionary in his own sense, a man who led his hapless people in a struggle that seemed hopelessly imbalanced in terms of power and magnitude. Mahasweta Devi re-invents the man who fought from the wrong side of history and geography, who led his men and women in a many sided battle to scratch back the only habitat their entire race ever knew, from the clutches of an enterprising empire. Since Birsa knew his people like no one else and since he had had an education in letters and divinity, he devised the most potent strategy in order to liberate his people. He realised that his race needed to be freed not only from the clutches of the dikku and the alien sarkar but also from themselves; their own rites and rituals and other expensive traditions that served the only purpose of making their lives more burdened and perpetually indebted. He realised that the most potent weapon of mass mobilisation for his people was the attainment of Godhood and he alone could fill that space, and so he did, not to govern his people but to liberate them.

Mahashweta Devi showcases complete awareness of the evolution of the protagonist in the novel from an 'ordinary' boy born to poor and 'starving' Mundas to the self-acclaimed bhagwan of his people. It is widely believed that at Bandgaon he experienced a vision of Vishnu. Later Sing Bonga, the sun deity of Jharkhandi Kheroals, revealed himself to Birsa. It was also under the influence of such experiences that Birsa began to feel himself the messiah of his downtrodden people. Since his childhood Birsa had shown traits of unusual and extraordinary behaviour. He added to it by his education at various missionary schools though he began at the school of Jaipal Nag. His personality was constantly and gradually enriched by the inner stirrings that he is believed to have been experiencing for long. All these developments were made appropriately relevant to the unusual times as Mundas had been striving for the restoration of their rights. Birsa himself had been feeling the pain of subjugation in his own land. Therefore, his education, religious training, personal traits and the present day circumstances led to the 'assimilation of two powerful mindsets: messiahism and revolutionary activism'(Roycroft 56).

The novel locates Birsa Munda and the struggle of the Munda agitators, known as sardars, in the historical background. They had been long in search of an iconic figure in order to mobilise the mass population in their struggle for their rights over their age old resources of forests. Once during vacation from the missionary school, Birsa was approached by Dhani Munda, an accomplice of the sardars who lamented that the 'bhagwan hasn't appeared yet."

"The Bhagwan from amongst the Mundas, who will win the mulkai ladai for us."

"Then?"

"He will rid our land of the sahibs and the dikku. He will restore the kingdom of the Mundas once again."

"But why are you telling me?"

"Birsa you can do it. Chotanagpur belongs to your ancestors. You could be bhagwan" (71).

Invocation of the forefathers' universal and unquestionable rights over the lands and forests of Chotanagpur by the Bhagwan Birsa thus became a war cry of the Ulgulan later on: 'sirmare firun raja jai' (victory to the ancestral kings). After he left the mission, Dhani attempted once more to convince Birsa to accept his pending godhood and tried to dissuade him from joining the Vaishnavite Anand Pandey at Bandgaon. Dhani almost commanded, despairingly, "I say come at once Birsa, and be the Bhagwan of the Mundas. You are born a Munda. Look after them" (79).

As mentioned earlier, when he finally returned as Bhagwan, he announced to his mother, "My people wanted a Bhagwan, mother I have returned as one" (92). Birsa's godhood has been a subject of ridicule amongst the Imperial historians. Mahasweta Devi's account deflates the imperialist bias and explains the facts that compel Birsa Munda to accept godhood.

The element of religious rujuvenation, backed by militant approach is a consistent feature of most of the peasant and tribal uprisings that have come to light from the colonial period (Spivak 131) Writing about the hool Ranajit Guha mentions, "Religiosity was, by all accounts, central to the hool. The notion of power which inspired it, was made up of such ideas and expressed in such words and acts as were explicitly religious in character. It was not that power was a content wrapped up in a form external to it called religion. It was matter of both being inseparably collapsed as the signified and the signifier... Hence the attribution of the rising to a divine command" (Guha 34).

It is thus to the credit of Mahashweta Devi for portraying an almost reluctant' bhagwan that Birsa was till he annonced himself to be one. But once he realised himself to be fully prepared for such a role there was no looking back on it. But throughout the evolution to such a level and, in the backdrop of desperate need and the compulsions of the circumstances, plenty of room is left for interpretation of Birsa's Godhood, a phenomenon which seems almost inevitable. Arnold writes about the historical and universal nature of such a process:

As in many other parts of the world where a traditional society has found itself under attack from aggressive modern imperialism and capitalism, the reaction of the hillmen took various forms. Arnold explains that religious element played a very important role at such moments. The reaction encapsulated various such fears and expectations in religious terms. Arnold explains that, "... religious idiom gave the hillmen a framework within which to conceptualize their predicament and to seek solution to it. Religion...provided a basis for solidarity against outsiders (141).

Secondly, there was always the possibility of a strong provoked method of retaliation which Arnold explains as, 'crime-as-protest element. Since the aggrieved felt wronged by the oppressor, therefore even individual instances of crime were seen as, "...defiance against all outsiders and oppressors. Ambivalence best describes this fluidity between crime and protest" (Arnold 141).

Where religion galvanises solidarity among the followers of a particular movement and fosters brotherhood, the element of crime not only expresses defiance, but more importantly, it shows desperation on the part of the insurgents in the face of the overwhelming enemy and reveals the futility of any other method apart from that of violence. The Birsaites also took to violence quite late in the movement, also learning from the frustrating experiences of the past when no one took notice of their peaceful petitions. Two other texts that correspond to this phenomenon are Chinua Achebe's Things Fall Apart (1958) and Gopinath Mohanty's Paraja (1945) where towards the end of each novel, the protagonists, Okonkwo and Mandia Jani, slaughter the colonial official and the zamindar respectively, the personified forces of exploitation. It was the only method of protest they felt they were left with.

Subaltern historiography is loaded with examples of the political and social movements that were disguised in the religious garb. The Devi movement of southern Gujarat in November 1922 resembles Birsa's call for Ulgulan except that in the former case the 'leader' was a...mata or a devi known as Salabhai...who expressed her thoughts through spirit mediums... By December some new commands of the Devi began to be heard.

Salabhai was telling the adivasis to take vows in Gandhi's name, to wear khadi cloth and to attend nationalist schools" (Hardiman 56), The Tana Bhagat movement of the oraons of Chotanagpur of almost the same period is another example of the role of the religious element in such popular movements.

Birsa Munda's Ulgulan was, however, different. Here was a leader in the human form who had 'declared' himself Bhagwan to lead his people out of the shackles of slavery, humiliation and exploitation.

Another peculiar trend present almost universally in all such movements, whether or not with a religious flavor, was that of the rumour as "a means of communication...in the mobilization of insurgency (Spivak 351). Spivak further explains why rumour should have played such an important role and suggests it was due to, "...its functional immediacy and its non-belonging to any one voice- consciousness. This is supposed to be the signal characteristic of writing. Any reader can 'fill' it with her 'consciousness' Rumour evokes comradeship because it belongs to every 'reader' or 'transmitter'. No one is its origin or source... [its] illegitimacy makes it accessible to insurgency" (353).

Rycroft (2004) too stresses on the role of 'rumours' in spreading the message of Birsa Bhagwan. The sardars were behind such rumours as he writes, "Rumours of Birsa's miraculous and prophetic qualities were disseminated by the sardars to foster and mobilize sentiment against the missions and the Raj authorities." The news spread alarmingly across all the villages with people in ecstatic mood crying, "Birsa is Bhagwan. He will cure the sick and feed the hungry" (Aranyar

Adhikar 92). Mahashweta Devi writes, "Birsa is now Dharti Aba. They had waited for someone like him for too long- the one who could wage a war against the missionaries and Sing Bonga alike. Sing Bonga was no more capable of protecting his people. They no longer felt safe in the lap of Jesus. They had wanted new God- the one who wouldn't mislead about the superstitions of ghosts and spirits or about the kingdom of Heaven. They just wanted the one who could end the reign of the dikku and the sarkar" (94).

Birsa and the Ulgulan probably owe much to the effort of the sardars and the other followers in propagating such mass communication which enabled him to mobilize his people for the movement against the administration. Mahasweta Devi mentions about such possibilities prevalent in those circumstances, "Birsa noted the movements of the sky, earth and the jungle and predicted the famine of 1895-96 Only Birsaites would survive... Birsa will usher in a new age. We will work hard then. Stop all work for the time being as it is going to benefit only the dikku and their sirkar. Sardars spread the message - Bhagwan is warning of doom. Don't sow new crops. Stop payment of revenue to the sirkar. Consume all your grains' (96). Then the author comments, "...some Mundas became ecstatic while some worried. But no one tried to find out whether it was Bhagwan or the sardars who had issued those instructions"(96).

Irrespective of the source of the warnings, it may be noted that warnings were common with the rumours in most such mobilizations Jitu Santal's followers, during the uprising in Malda in north western Bengal, spread warnings through rumours about people becoming blind or contracting cholera upon non-compliance and, on the other hand the fruits of self-Raj upon obediance of instructions (Sarkar 152). Also, while mobilising support for the fituris (uprisings) in the Godavari region, rumour mongers issued severe threats to the muttadars (petty landlord chieftans) into joining the uprisings (Arnold 126).

The author provides amplc space to the process of introspection that Birsa often involved himself in. Soon after he announced himself to be Dharti Aba, he toured from village to village teaching people how to fight against various diseases such as cholera. Birsa knew that he had no magical cure to rid people of these diseases except inculcating among people some basic habits of cleanliness and hygeine which he had learnt at the mission school. Still his people believed that those fatal diseases just vanished in the company of Bhagwan. The author shows that Birsa had realised that spreading the message of his new religion [wherein he taught his followers to abandon numerous expensive rites, rituals and sacrifices] - preventing the epidemics from spreading far and wide- that alone will not make him the real Dharti Aba. Whatever he had done so far was the result of his education at the mission school and even of the Vaishnavite ashram and of his experiences of the last six years. The author writes,

He knew that he will have to play the other role as well... Also Birsa realised that the sardars were instrumental in spreading rumours about his divine powers to meet their own ends since they knew

people have faith in him. He did not want to be a puppet in their hands but wanted to a leader in his own way" (101-104).

With this realisation begins the final phase of Birsa's life. Under his leadership the Mundas began to disobey the administrative system. The zamindars became anxious over the colossal loss of revenue, Sardars came in flocks to join the war cry - *Ulgulan.* The administrative machinery too got nervous fearing such disobedience to be the preparation for some rebellion. They were absolutely clueless about who enthused Mundas with such confidence. The sahibs at the missionaries got alarmed and their anxiety resulted in direct police action against Birsa. Their first attempt on 9th August failed due to the resistance by Birsa's father and family, who outnumbered Luchman Lal (Head Constable of Tamar Police Station) and his two officers.... Following rumours that the Birsaites were threatening to massacre all non- Birsaite dikku, Rev. Lusty reported Birsa's perceived criminality to G.RK. Meares, the Ranchi District Superintendent of Police. Birsa's retreat at Chalkad was subjected to surveillance. About his night time capture on August 23 1895, K.S. Singh cites Meares: "The Sub-inspector from Khunti...entered Birsa's room [where] he was found asleep, his body smeared with turmeric. He struggled violently when handcuffs were slipped on his wrists.. Birsa was then taken out and marched away without any trouble" (Singh 1983: 67).

Meares later suggested to the Lieutenant Governor that Birsa be declared mad in order to shake his followers' faith in him. It was Dr. Rogers, much to Meares' dismay, who refused to oblige, citing that Birsa was not mad and that even Christ claimed to have supernatural powers without necessarily being mad. Later Birsa was tried in public so the images of his subjugation and taming might 'expose' his fraudulent claim to his followers. He was sentenced to two years in prison.

Christian missionaries play an important role in the lives of the Mundas, like all other tribals in those belts. There are, however, differing views on the exact role of the missionaries in their lives. After Birsa's first arrest, Roycroft maintains, many Birsaites reconverted to Christianity for the fear of retribution (59). Later, he refers to Singh (1983) who writes that after Operation Salrakar of 1900, while Birsa fled into the forests, most of his followers reconverted into Christianity fearing the police's 'reign of terror' (60). In a very signigicant way Mahasweta Devi, however, takes a very different line of interpretation. The novel suggests that the Mundas became very pragmatic and in order to survive for the two years without their Bhagwan and to be safe from hunger, joining the mission was the best possible option before them. She writes," the Mundas flocked to reconvert into Christianity. Dhani said, "Why not? It is important to survive for two years. We will see then" (129). It was not unusual for people to convert to Christianity in difficult times.

Earlier in the novel, hearing about the strange things Birsa was involved in, in the jungle, Sugana gave him the secret of survival of the Mundas as he told his son, "Be like the other boys Birsa. Become a Christian when there is a famine or a disease. And on harvesting a good crop, return to your own religion"(46). The author suggests that this was the commonly followed method of survival for those who were either not too sure of their own religion and yet wanted to survive in hostile conditions and those who just saw it as an easy way of life since the missionaries provided many comforts that were beyond the reach of an average Munda.

After his release from the prison in 1897 Birsa began to infuse life in Ulgulan once again. Meanwhile the sardars had managed to keep his divinity alive in the popular memory. Birsaites began with new enthusiasm- Sirmai firun raja jai, ghartir pudoi raja jai - victory to the heaven king, victory to the earth king (Dharti Aba) Detailed plans were chalked out for the restoration of the kingdom of the Mundas. Birsa offered his followers the twin ways of war or peace. The sardars rejected the path of peace as it meant filing more applications to the government, something they had been doing for decades.

The bloody war resulted in the form of Operation Salrakar on 9th January 1900 in which non-government sources quote some four hundred Mundas were massacred including women and children. This followed the attack on the state establishment on the Christmas eve by the Birsaites. Soon after Salrakar, sarkar began to isolate Birsaites and punish them. Birsa was caught by the police with the help of Shashi Bhushan Rai and six other Mundas for the monetary award of five hundred rupees. Four hundred and eighty two other Birsaites were arrested along with him, of which only eighty were tried.

Birsa died in jail of Asiatic cholera though it is believed that he was poisoned either by the police or the sardars who feared Birsa might reveal their plans (Roycroft 60).

Birsa was all of twenty five when he was declared dead, of Asiatic Cholera as per the superintendent Anderson's report even though the symptoms defied such certification. The government was in a hurry to see the end of Birsa and his Ulgulan. In the first few pages of the novel the subtext hints at the gaps and the lapses in the official view of the incidence. The relevance of qui parle is manifested in the subdued argument that goes on between the British Superintendent of prison, Anderson and his Indian deputy Amulya, a young Bengali who had been an orphan at Ranchi and was for sometime a class fellow of Birsa at the German missionary school at Chaibasa.

Anderson believed it was Amulya who leaked the news of the Ulgulan to the newspapers in Calcutta but had no proof to substantiate his claim. Anderson was also irritated at Amulya's sympathy with the prisoners and his regular references to the Jail Code Book. Though Birsa had died in the morning of ninth June but his body was inspected only after five thirty in the evening. Later in the evening Amulya met him in connection with the last rites of Birsa. "Will his brother Kanu light the pyre?," Amulya Babu asked. "O no! Not at all. If Birsaites witness the cremation, they will spread rumours about it. They will spread that he was cremated with honour. They will fish out anecdotes about him. I..I can not hear more such things about Birsa," replied Anderson. Anderson tried to pacify a visibly upset Amulya." It does not befit you to accept such things. You are an educated person. You belong to our religion. Look I have been sick of listening to anecdotes about him for years...but now, he had been in this very jail even before. You too saw he was an ordinary man, an ordinary Munda, so what what if he died of cholera...?"

"Shall we wash his cell with carbolic?"
"Carbolic? Why? Have you gone mad?"
"But sir, cholera is infectious, isn't it?"
"Cholera? How on earth did you remember cholera?"
"You said Birsa died of cholera."

Anderson's jaws shook for a while. And then he said rudely, "Yes, it was I who said it- Birsa died of cholera. I say I don't understand where he contracted it. 1 say there is no need to wash his cell with carbolic. I say that he will be cremeted by the jail employees. Not a single Birsaite should get to see his cremation- note it - not a single one of them should be able to get there. On seeing it they will spread rumours and anecdotes of him, and Jacob will blame us for humiliating that unfortunate Munda's corpse by forcing the prisoners to witness his cremation. Is it clear now?" (Aranyar Adhikar 16-18).

From the conversation between Amulya and Anderson, it is abundantly clear that Birsa may not have died of cholera. Were one to see the official version of his death, there will not be a shade of suspicion in it. Here the author, with her indepth research and a sense of responsibility to portray the truth, attempts to paint a just picture of the events and circumstances that led to the untimely death of Birsa Munda. Though Amulya Babu was a part of the administrative machinery, he had his sympathies with the rebels because he identified with them as an orphan himself. Also, he had spent a few formative years of his life in the company of Birsa. Amulya was not alone who sympathised with the rebel cause. Barrister Jacob was another. Though he was British, he fought all the cases on the behalf of the Mundas without charging any fee.

The efforts of Birsa did not go waste though. Ulgulan did not end, Bhagwan does not die (*Aranyar Adhikar* 18). When Amulya lamented that Birsa's rebellion was rendered futile, Barrister Jacob consoled him saying, 'Whether all the wars or rebellions were wasted or realised is a complex matter that can not be evaluated' (243). It is acknowledged that it was the rebellion of Birsa and many others that the tribal leaders had led before and after him that resulted in the Chotanagpur Tenancy Act of 1908 which marked the beginning of the restoration of the rights of the tribal people, a process that is yet not complete, fulfilling gradually the promise that Birsa made to his followers, 'Our time has come. I will restore your land to you. Our fields shall not have boundaries. We will all cultivate collectively. No Munda will own anything in the private capacity There shall be no wars and there will be the reign of religion' (159).

The representation of Birsa Munda in the novel is based on reality and the novelist did ample research before venturing on writing the novel. The novel, though written by a member of the mainstream society, a non-tribal, but it offers the viewpoint of the Mundas pitted against not only the Imperial regime but the dominant Indian community as well.

Works Cited:

Achebe, Chinua. Things Fall Apart. 1958. New York: Anchor Books, 1994. Print.

Alam, Javeed. "Fragmented Culture and Strangulated Existence: Jharkhand's Cultural Encounter with the Modern". Continuity and Change in Tribal Society, Ed. Mrinal Miri. Shimla: IIAS, 1993, Print.

Arnold, David. "Rebellious Hillmen: The Gudem Rampa Risings 1839-1924". Subaltern Studies: Writings on South Asian History and Society. 1982. Ed. Ranajit Guha. Vol. I. New Delhi: OUP, 2005. Print.

Dasgupta, Sangeeta. "Recasting the Oraons and the 'Tribe' Sarat Chandra Roy's Anthology" (132-171) Anthropology in the East: Founders of Indian Sociology and Anthropology Eds. Patricia Uberoi et al. Ranikhet: Permanent Black, 2007. Print.

Deshpande, Satish et al, eds. Introduction. Anthropology in the East: Founders of Indian Sociology and Anthropology Ranikhet: Permanent Black, 2007. Print

Devi, Mahasweta. Aranyar Adhikar. 1977. Trans. Jagat Shankhdhar, Jangal Ke Davedar. New Delhi: Radhakrishan, 2008. Print.

Ekka, Philip. "Revivalist Movements Among the Tribals of Chotanagpur" (395-402). The Tribal Situation in India 1972. Ed. K Suresh Singh. Shimla: IIAS, 2002. Print.

Fernandes, Walter "Informal Economy, Dependence and Management Traditions" (48-69). Continuity and Change in Tribal Society. Ed. Mrinal Miri. Shimla: Indian Institute of Advanced Study, 1993. Print

Guha, Ranajit. "The Prose of Counter-Insurgence" (1-42). Subaltern Studies, 1983. Ed. Ranajit Guha. Vol. II. New Delhi: OUP, 2005. Print.

_ _ _ _. "Discipline and Mobilize" (68-120), Subaltern Studies, 1992. Ed. Partha Chatterjee and Gyanendra Pandey, Vol. VII. New Delhi: OUP, 2005, Print.

Hardiman, David. "Adivasi Assertion in South Gujarat: The Devi Movement of 1922-3" (57-94). Histories of the Subordinated. New Delhi: Permanent Black, 2006. Print.

Linkenback, Antje. Forest Futures: Global Representations and Ground Realities in the Himalayas. Ranikhet: Permanent Black, 2007. Print.

Roycroft, Daniel J. "Capturing Birsa Munda: The Virtiality of a Colonial- era Photograph." Indian Folklore Research Journal, Vol. 1, No. 4, 2004: 53- 68. Print

Saldanha, Indra Munshi. "Customary Rights and Colonial Regulations: Thana Forests in the Nineteenth Century" (70-84). Continuity and Change in Tribal Society. Ed. Mrinal Miri. Shimla: Indian Institute of Advanced Study. 1993. Print.

Sarkar, T. "Jitu Santal's Movement in Malda, 1924-1932: A Study in Tribal Protest" (136-164). Subaltern Studies. 1985. Ed. Ranajit Guha. Vol. IV. New Delhi: Oxford UP, 2005. Print.

Sarkar, M.C. "Customary Rights in Land and Forest of the Tribals in Chotanagpur- Santhal Pargana Region of Bihar" (97-108). Continuity and Change in Tribal Society. Ed. Mrinal Miri. Print.

Singh, K.S. "Agrarian Issues in Chotanagpur" (347-359). The Tribal Situation in India, 1972. Ed. K Suresh Singh. Shimla: IIAS, 2002. Print.

_ _ _ _. Birsa Munda and His Movement 1874-1901. A Study of a Millenarian Movement in Chotanagpur. 1966. Calcutta: OUP, 1983. Print.

Skaria, Ajay. "Writing, Orality and Power in the Dangs, Western India, 1800s - 1920s (13-58). Subaltern

Studies. 1996. Ed. Shahid Amin and Dipesh Chakrabarty. Vol. IX. New Delhi: OUP, 2005. Print

Spivak, Gayatri Chakravorty. "A Literary Representation of the Subaltern: Mahasweta Devi's 'Stanadayini'" (91-134). Subaltern Studies. 1987. Ed. Ranajit Guha. Vol. V. New Delhi: OUP, 2005. Print.

_ _ _ _. "Subaltern Studies: Deconstructing Historiography" (330-363). Subaltern Studies. 1985. Ed. Ranajit Guha. Vol. IV. Print.

Chapter - 5

Billy Biswas and 'His' Tribals

I came a thousand miles to see your face,
O mountain,
A thousand miles did I come to see your face!

(A bhil song, The Strange Case of Billy Biswas 7)

Arun Joshi's *The Strange Case of Billy Biswas* is primarily about the estranged protagonist Billy Biswas and his destiny that finds itself struggling between two very different and varying surrounding, one was the 'civilised' and metropolitan Delhi that he never can cope with therefore disowns, and the other, the world of the tribals of the Maikala hills in Madhya Pradesh, that he longs for but is hardly allowed to embrace for too long. The novel provides the plain reader a gripping story of someone who is dissatisfied with his life in the civilised world and is unaffected by his comfortable place in it. The protagonist is not content with this mere "dissatisfaction' and revolts in the only way he knew, that is, by quitting it altogether. Where the new world of his accepts him without too many questions and reservations, his old world does not quite forget him and then claims him even at the cost of his life.

The themes that are dealt with in the novels of Arun Joshi are of universal nature. The disappearance of the protagonist and his subsequent settlement in the tribal world is attempted. As a critic has rightly observed,

"The problem of oppression and the oppressed, the victims and the victimizers have deeply agitated the modern and the post modern writers all over the world. The individual is safe and free only if he fights back the evils of the political and tyrannical forces of the Society. Arun Joshi points the direction, presents the problem but does not show a real authentic, realistic way out" (Alexander 98).

The case of this man called Billy (Bimal) Biswas is 'strange' for it does not fit into the accepted norm of the 'civilised society and Billy finds himself motivated enough to rebel and thus break its shackles to join a world that is far removed from the everyday reality of his former world and therefore, The Strange Case of Billy Biswas is the only novel of Arun Joshi which creates an aesthetic sign of the mythical orality of a tribal world against the sterility of contemporary technological mechanics of human values' (Dhawan 194).

The novel The Strange case of Billy Biswas was published in 1971. This novel is a statement of Joshi's fictional art which is strikingly different from his contemporaries. 'While Anita Desai and Kamala Markandaya concentrate on the social scenario and endeavour to underline its inadequacies, Joshi explores the individual psyche of the protagonist' (Vachaspati 87).

Billy was a man of extraordinary sensibilities, and in many ways, very different from the other men and women around him. He desired something that not many people spend time thinking about. It can be said that his was a unique search for the finer elements of life and he chased his greater pursuits by taking some very unusual decisions that made substantial difference not just to his life but to the life of everyone else around him as Mallikarjun Patil is tempted to note. "Billy Biswas is a Gandhian as far as his understanding of the present civilization goes; a Wordsworthian as he finds happiness in tribal life of simplicity and grace" (142).

Billy was a man of not just extraordinary sensibilities but also 'extraordinary obsessions' (7). He drifted towards a calling in his life that led his life into the sphere of 'strangeness'. He responded to what he himself mentioned as, " before the eye of each one of us, sooner or later, at one time of life or another, a phantom appears. Some, awed, pray for it to withdraw. Others, ostrich like, bury their heads in sand. There are those, however, who can do naught but grapple with such faceless tempters and chase them to the very ends of the earth "(7-8).

Billy chose to grapple with such faceless tempters and chased them to the very end of the earth, and that end he found amongst the tribal population living deep in the Maikala hills. The question that arises is what exactly did this faceless tempter propose to the protagonist? The answer is not too difficult to locate as it is hidden inside the 'dark depths' of 'incongruity of his eyes' (10). Billy wanted to find and live the true meaning of life. He was the one who was suffocated with what life in the metropolitan world, with all its security, had to offer him. The narrator admits:

If life's meaning lies not in the glossy surfaces of our pretensions, but in those dark mossy labyrinths of the soul that languish forever, hidden from the dazzling light of the sun, then I do not know of any man who sought it more doggedly and, having received a signal, abandoned himself so recklessly to its call. In brief, I know of no other man who so desperately pursued the tenuous thread of existence to its bitter end... (8).

Billy often talked about the 'fascinating societies exist[ing] in India. His interests included the tribal people living in India, Verrier Elwin, the gond kings, and concepts of rituals and taboo. He would often talk about having had the glimpse of the other side of life, the valley beyond the hills; the hills beyond the valley. His woman friend from Sweden, Tuula, expressed to the narrator how Billy was possessed with, "A great force, urkraft, a... primitive force... which [could) explode any time"(18).

To some extent it goes to the credit of the tribal world and the tribal way of life and values, that a man of such exalted sensibilities, who, in order to search a meaning in life, and to live the essence of that meaning, should choose to live amidst them. However, with such an assertion, one is tempted to idolise and romanticise the primitive world, which has its own share of worries and sorrows.

According to the objective of the present study, of greater importance is to try to understand why Billy chose the tribal world for his pursuits. What was lacking in the metropolitan world that he abandoned and with it abandoned the rest of his family which included his parents, wife and his only son? What in the tribal world held fascination for him and what in that world facilitated his ambitions that his former world threatened to obstruct? Thereafter, it is important to study the portrayal of the tribal world in the novel as the story is concentrated entirely on Billy and his adventures. The tribal world, as represented in this novel by the inhabitants of the Maikala hills, as compared to metropolitan Delhi or even New York, was, simply put, simpler, quieter and consisted of, if not happier, then at least more real people. It was certainly a world that Billy would have called more 'human' as is indicated by his choice of living in Harlem in New York as it was the most human place he could find' since, 'White America was too civilized for him (9). It was in this world of the tribals that he found his mahaprasad (the greatest friend), both of whom could gladly die for each other.

Years later, after the narrator and Billy have met, Billy explains his new people and new life to Romi Saham. Billy describes the people there to Romi as, "....these people, which includes me now, are never really surprised at anything human. Mechanical things surprise them no end" (82). The people there didn't have any long term goals such as investments and education and the environment was marked by a complete absence of things such as political and religious institutions, social awareness, mass movements, transport, communication, markets etc. This probably suited Billy's temperament as he later told Romi, "Nobody here is interested in the price of food grains or new seeds or roads or elections, and stuff like that. We talk of the supernatural, violent death, trees, earth, rain, dust storm, and rivers, moods of the forests, animals, dance, and singing. And we talk, I am afraid, a lot about women and sex" (106). This was in sharp contrast to the civilization where much other preoccupation took the place of singing and dancing of the tribal world. The singing and dancing parties of the tribal society are so frequent and serve as one of the most important means of entertainment. In fact Nehru, as has already been mentioned in the study, admired them (the tribal people in general) for being so merry-making as compared to the majority of mainstream society the type of which sit in the stock exchanges all day and shout at each other and think themselves civilized (Guha 2008).

The novel depicts a tribal society that is not too much steeped in activities in order to amass wealth, material for comfort and other amenities. Of course, such realities are revealed to us through the protagonist of the novel during his conversations with the narrator. Billy described to Romi the life he had lived among the tribals as 'happy.' In his words, "We lived at the subsistence level... What kept us happy, I suppose, were the same thing that have kept all primitives happy through the ages, the earth, the forest, the rainbows, the liquor from the mahua, an occasional feast, a lot of dancing and lovemaking, and, more than anything else, no ambition, none at all" (107).

On the economic scale, however, this might be a society that will be labeled as backward, poor, lacking resources and opportunities but analyzing the society closely enough, it will be revealed that this society does not really demand much else. They produce enough food to last them a year. They have plenty of dance, music, wine and other such sensual engagements to keep them amused while they are not working. This is also revealed through the details that are provided in the novel. Billy himself came in close contact with Bilasia during one such nocturnal thrill of dance, music, wine and lovemaking. Parties of men and women, tired after a day of hard work, came from various villages to gather at some place to a night long session of merry making and leave in the early hours of the morning.

This impression of tribal society steeped in perpetual celebrations might mislead one into believing that there are no ills in that social set-up and everyone is happy and contended. To a large extent it could be concluded that they are in a way satisfied since the resources accessible to them are sufficient to meet their demands and they do not leave too much to be desired, Beneath this there is indeed a great deal of suffering since sometimes agricultural product is barely sufficient to feed them all the year. In addition to this drought plays major role since it prevails for a considerable part of the year, particularly the pre-monsoon period. It is the ritual of producing food grains and sustaining their bodies that keeps the tribal population occupied most of the time It is throughout this process that the people regularly organize events of mass entertainment and celebrations. This alone, as everywhere else, should not be thought of as sufficient to keep people happy all the time. Billy tells Romi, "It is amazing how unhappy everyone really is, even here" (106). This statement says more than many pages of study or years of observation could reveal. Billy left the mainstream world that he was born into in the hope of living a more meaningful life in more human surroundings. It was a journey from those who 'squandered the priceless treasure of life on that tinsel passed for civilization' (102) to live among those 'who are the inheritors of the cosmic light' (88).

In this novel, written by an outsider and a non-tribal the primary place is occupied by the non-tribal characters. It is also suggested by the title since the novel deals with the strange case of one Billy Biswas. Though his story would be incomplete without the involvement of the tribal characters, there are, not many of them in the novel Apart from the tribal characters there are many non-tribal characters other than the narrator, Meena Chatterjee, Rima Kaul, Romi Sahai, Situ, Billy's parents, Tuula and even some of the other minor characters are known by their names such as George, Mr. Kundt and so on.

As far as characters from the tribal world are concerned, there are just two who are important-Dhunia who is the mahaprasad of the protagonist and the other is Bilasia who become Billy's second wife and the mother of his children. Other than these two, there are many who are present all around but are never mentioned by their names. They are just mentioned as part of the dance party or drunks and anything else but by their names. Some of them play important role in keeping Billy's presence among them a secret and not succumbing to pressure from the police and administration. Despite the important role they play by proving to be honest and selfless, they have no names.

Dhunia is the first major (male) character from the tribal world who is introduced in the novel. Billy and he, having spent reasonably enough time in each other's company soon get into a relationship which is given the status of mahaprasad (the greatest friend). These two are the greatest friends of each other and each shall gladly sacrifice his life for the other if need be. Initially Billy gave them his company and sometunes antibiotic tablets to cure them of common diseases and in turn was helped by Dhunia by providing them ropes and other such things when Billy came there with his group of students from Delhi on archaeological expeditions.

Initially though, Romi and everyone else from Billy's former world probably held the tribals responsible for enticing Billy even though Romi knew Billy well and having some understanding of circumstances of Billy's life, didn't thereafter see things in the same light. Initially Romi too thought that the inhabitants of the protagonist's new world had some role to play in his strange adventures which finally rested in their lot. He mentions,

...and around these paths lay the widely scattered villages of India's primitive people the baigas, the gonds, the pardhans, and several others. Before coming I had read about them and talked to experts in Delhi. But sitting there I felt as ignorant of them as Rama who, too, had once trekked down through these same hills from the imperial city of Ayodhaya. I felt ignorant and quite a bit more helpless. All I knew was that they had done something fearful, something unspeakable, to this

*friend of mine so that, as the night advanced, 1
wondered where Billy Biswas I had known ended,
and whispering of the jungle began (77).*

Portrayal of the tribals (in the novel under study) is
marked by the characteristic elitism of the English
language which hampers a genuinely comprehensive
description of them. The novel maintains 'distance'
from the characters that it describes. It pins the tribal
character into a position, allowing little
maneuverability, and then observes it from several
corners. This limited space denies the characters the
power to demonstrate their strength of character and
conviction (that is, if they have any). In the literary
sense, the subaltern tribal characters are robbed off their
power of self-determination, and English language may
have some role in it, even though unintentionally.

Some might argue that the unbiased author is
simply portraying what can be observed in reality as the
presence of the characters from the mainstream society
renders the tribals relatively ineffective, passive and
submissive. Also, Spivak outrules the necessity of
representation to be carried out only by the group
people themselves as, "The position that only the
subaltern can know the subaltern, only women can
know women, and so on can not be held as a theoretical
presupposition either, for it predicates the possibility of
knowledge on identity" (235). This argument is not
without an element of truth. The overwhelming burden
that the tribals feel in the presence of people from the
outside world, especially in the presence of government
officials, is too visible in fiction written in regional

languages as well. However, in fiction written in the English language there is a 'veil' that separates the narrative and the characters, and the two are engaged only in segregated compartments and not as a cohesive whole.

In Joshi's *The Strange Case of Billy Biswas*, the tribals are secondary, disposable, inconsequential and conveniently forgettable. Since the narrative focuses on the protagonist, the characters from the tribal world are called upon to serve the theme and are discarded when their service is done. Some of the incidents in which the tribal characters are involved in decision-making (though rare) are brushed aside without any elaborate description and their lot comes across as faceless and those who do not decide their own fate. Though it can be established in reality that the lesser privileged in the society are not allowed to decide their own fate by those who are materialistically developed but even when it is about deciding their personal matters and choices, the tribals are shown as incapable, slavish and indifferent.

The characters from the tribal world serve the main world of the civilized as objects of passive participation, and they are placed in a secondary position in relation to the protagonist and the main characters of the novels. They form the background and their involvement or role at best serves the development of the main plot, the main characters or the main theme. As an independent entity, the tribal world sits as nothing but a silent spectator to the ongoing drama. In fact in most cases it is seen or projected as a living being dwelling in the remote areas on the outskirts of the civilized humanity and is needed by it as an accessory for the purpose of decoration, amusement and recreation.

The mainstream world glorifies the tribal social system but at the same time subjugates it to its mainstream powerful value system in a very damaging and a humiliating way. In The Strange Case of Billy Biswas, the tribals shudder at the name and sight of the District Collector and the other officials. They address these officers as their mai-baap (parents) and call themselves their children. Also, in Gopinath Mohanty's Orissa classic Paraja, the officials of the government such as the forest guard and the police cause acute terror in the hearts of the tribal people. The tribals have to give in to the will of this official unless they are prepared for the consequences. Therefore, their independence is limited and they are only truly independent when they are not in touch with the officials of the government. It thus goes that his rhetoric to glorify the otherwise realistic tribals, helps the mainstream society to provide a smokescreen under which a whole lot of exploitation and corruption take place.

Moreover, the tribal characters are not represented as individuals but as the part of a 'collective tribal character' where homogeneity prevails as a rule. Any tribal character in the narrative is supposed to be just like the other, clubbed together as a uniform regiment. This invariably gives rise to stereotypes, leading to gross generalisation about the behaviour, thinking and attitudes of the tribals contributing to a misleading picture of the tribal people. Representation of the tribals in fiction by way of characterisation posits the problem of othering' of the subversive peripherising of the tribal. As far as the tribal characterisation is concerned, the tribals form a collective lot that need not be imparted individual traits but must collectively serve to reveal or express the character of the protagonist or the other leading character in the novel. In Arun Joshi's The Strange Case of Billy Biswas, Bilasia, her uncle Dhunia and the other characters are useful in enlightening the readers about Billy's character, his nature, actions and destiny. At one point in the novel, Billy's friend Romesh Sahai, the district collector talks to Dhunia about Billy's 'strange' conduct.

Can you tell me, Dhunia… Why do you think he did such an odd thing? I mean why did he leave us?'

'You make fun of me, collector sahib… how could I, a poor man, who cannot even write his name, tell you, the king of the district, why he did what he did' (115).

The conversation continues. Romesh Sahai, the district collector and a friend to Billy Biswas and Dhunia, are both involved in finding and revealing reasons, respectively, for the strange behavior of the protagonist. Interestingly, both are seen to be doing the same thing but the difference is appalling. The district collector may have been a close friend of Billy but then so is Dhunia. Romesh Sahai is projected to be standing on a platform much higher than the tribal Dhunia, not necessarily because the former is an official, 'the king of the district' as Dhunia calls him but because the former carries the authority of belonging to the civilized world and Dhunia carries the apology, regret and the mental stigma of the tribal world.

Dhunia can never imagine to share with Romesh Sahar a platform, where both are seen as equals. Notwithstanding the fact that Dhunia is both Mahaprasad (the greatest friend) and almost the father-in-law of Billy, he is still seen as the one pleading before Romesh Sahai. It may be argued that Romesh Sahai was the district collector and it was 'natural' for frightened tribal to be pleading before the officials even though not guilty of any crime. At the same time it can be stated very unambiguously that even if Billy's first wife Meena's father had come asking Dhunia for his son-in-law, Dhunia would have been presented in the same poor light. Dhunia, in terms of the relationship with Billy, is superior or more advanced than Meena's father for he, in addition to being Billy's father-in-law like Mr. Chatterjee (Meena's father) is also Billy's Mahaprasad (the greatest friend), a position that only Romesh Sahai could compete with. However, Dhunia would have been delineated as the 'lesser one' for he belongs to a world, that, in comparison to the mainstream world, understands its relatively low position and is visibly apologetic about it.

One characteristic of the tribal society that is blown out of proportion is their "submissive indifference' to things happening around them. When Billy decides to go back to the civilized' world that he had left, no one complains. The tribal community simply accepts it as if they have no emotion, no mind and no point of view of their own. Oh the contrary, when, Billy left the former world, the family cried, the press voiced its concern and the administration and the police tried to find him. But when Billy willingly decides to leave the tribal world no one voices any concern.

Billy had not just been accepted as one of them but also their leader and mahaprasad by Dhunia. Had he disappeared suddenly they would have taken him to have been eaten up by a man-eater tiger. Only Bilasia protests against his decision. She is anyway presented as sensual though faithful. She could be understood as 'just another tribal girl', wine drinking, merry making and a love-maker's delight. What surprises the reader is that when Billy is killed no one utters a word. Not a syllable! They are not shown as too shocked to say anything but as too dumb to express their view, if they have one at all. It's just Dhunia who asys something. Dhunia asys, "So you killed him, collector sahib, he sobbed.... You are mother and our father, and you killed him. But Bhagwan sees all. He will see that justice is done" (170). It is a pity that the position of the tribals is demeaned to such an extent that despite the killing of their leaders, Dhunia, the tribal headman does not forget the 'fact that the district collector is the mai baap of the tribals. It is appalling that Dhunia should express his tribute to the collector who is representation of the cruel, savage and the "civilized' world that first set into the confines of the world to fish out the one who had willingly chosen to live there and in the process killed him.

The other possibility, however, could be that the author was making an attempt to focus upon the strength of the tribal headman Dhunia who maintains his calm and composure under great adversity and does not falter like an ordinary mortal. But the fact one cannot overlook in this context is that even under such adverse circumstances the tribal headman Dhunia dose not forget his subaltern position in relation to the civilised world and he must express humility, gratitude and apology no matter he has been a recipient of injustice from the civilised world.

Thus it could be very well argued that the English fiction falls much short of diving right into the tribal world and seeing everything through their eyes and perspective. On the other hand it does just the opposite, ie, it appropriates the tribals setting into that of its own mainstream plot and then presents the tribal world in such a manner that it seems rootless, alien, superstitions and unwanted. It is wanted. It is wanted only as long as it helps further the main story and the characterisation of the protagonist and other characters who are necessarily from the non-tribal, sophisticated and the so called civilised world.

It is possibly because Indian writing is English is created, influenced and continued by "dominant minority" as Nirad C. Chaudhary puts it (Furer-Haimendorf, 313). Though there have been notable exceptions such as R.K. Narayan and Raja Rao; the majority of writers - men as well as women have preferred to create worlds in the fictions that do not resemble or represent the cultural ethos, value system and sensibilities of the majority, be it urban, rural or tribal.

Here, for example, is a contrast between the portrayal of the two wives of Billy Biswas. One is Meena Chatterjee from the civilized world. She, as a modern society wife, claims a lot of attention and right over Billy and his world, so much so that the two begin to quarrel over it. When Billy gets too busy with his work it is she who protests and tries to make Billy guilty of neglecting her. On the other hand, Bilasia, Billy's second wife and from the tribal society accepts her position as a 'wife' and is shown to be indifferent to her sorrows and joys. Not much of their conversation is given much importance except that of the beginning which is mostly lusty and about merry making. The author does not pay must attention to about what and how Billy and she would have discussed their day to day things. She is absent mindedly presented as an unquestioning, subdued and a subjected wife who probably never dared to see herself as an equal player in matrimony. Her equality with her husband was only limited to drinking, smoking, dancing and merry-making with him. She is presented as incapable of being involved mentally and emotionally. She works as a perfect instrument to keep Billy happy and be available whenever he needs her. She only makes some protest when Billy decides to go back to his former world. Other than that her emotional requirements, her character traits and her psychological aspects are not really explored.

On the whole the author spends a lot of time and space describing the landscape, the customs and the rituals of the tribals. A large part of it is explained while revealing some or the other aspect of Billy's nature or development of character. During the conversation between Billy and Romesh (when they met after many years), the author, through the mind of Romesh in contemplation explains-

Beyond the gorge was a flat rocky strip of land across which I had, during the quiet of a night, heard the lusty laughter of men and women and had wondered where they went at that time of night. Beyond this strip of land was the jungle, a dark and mysterious shadow whose mystery very few collectors had unraveled since the race of collectors began. It stretched on and on as the eye could see until it dissolved into what looked like a heap of storm clouds but which in reality were the low hills that formed an offshoot of the Maikala Range (77).

Much lesser attention or space is offered to the individual characters form the tribal world. They are clubbed together as a group of people sharing common nature.

They are supposed to be like one another. They are represented more as a common class than as individuals.

The tribal world of Billy Biswas may be accused of lying, which can easily be confirmed by the way Dhunia or his wife village folks lied about Billy without which he would have been found out without much inconvenience. What has to be seen here is whether Dhunia and his folk were naturally inclined to lie. He was, indeed, forced to tell a lie by none other than Dr. Birmal Biswas, a product of metropolitan and culturally rich Delhi and a doctorate in Archaeology from the United State of America. Dhunia's natural instincts would never have obliged Billy had he not felt compelled by his obligations towards his mahaprasad.

This natural truhfulness and obligation towards his worldly duty shown by Dhunia goes unnoticed in the eyes of a common reader, especially from the mainstream society, for whom he is just the bridge which facilitated Billy's madness and misdirected adventures. Dhunia is shown as servile, slavish and inevitably one of the types of underlings. In the novel his servility, as depicted by the author could be due to two reasons Dhunia being one of the tribals of course, was overawed by the administrative machinery and the agents of the superior and more powerful non-tribal system. Secondly, the author probably found it difficult to present his readers a tribal character who could talk to his administrative officers and police and be the greatest friend to one of their citizens from the mainstream world.

It was mentioned by the narrator, "He must have been a man of considerable influence among his own people, but behaved towards us especially towards the uniformed policeman- with a cloying servility that for me was greatly annoying even though, I suspect, it was mostly put on. He kept his hands folded all through our interview, refused to sit down, and denied anything, absolutely anything, that was asked!"(62). It is true that most of that servility was 'put on' in order to avoid being on the wrong side of things. It was not to obtain some favors from the authorities. His servility had a purpose and it was to show everything as normal and avoid any unnecessary trouble that might lead one to any information about Billy. When the collector Romi Sahai finally wanted to back the news of his having found Billy and wanted some information about him from Dhunia, he continued with his servile behavior even though he didn't reveal the whereabouts of Billy till he was told by the collector that he had come to know about Billy.

Towards the end of the novel when the 'misfired' shot killed Billy, the author shows Dhunia both as servile and respectful and also forgiving. On seeing dead who was once his 'greatest friend on earth', Dhunia says to Romi, 'so you killed him, collector sahib...you killed him. It is indeed strange to see that even in such a distressed moment when Dhunia should naturally have flown into a rage, he is shown as not forgetting to pay ample respect to Romi, the collector of the district, by calling him mai baap, though he does not forget to add, 'but Bhagwan sees all. He will see that justice is done'. Dhunia, by murdering the havildar who fired at Billy, finally took the revenge for the untimely death of his friend, who was to the tribal community 'like rain on parched lands, like balm on a wound (115). And by ignoring this information, Romi shares a platform with Dhunia where he too shares a secret satisfaction in avenging the death of his friend.

Therefore Dhunia, though shown as servile and cloying, comes out as elegant, truthful, uniquely bound by duty towards his mahaprasad and sometimes by being overawed by the administration and police and to play his 'role' (assigned indirectly by Billy) masterfully servile and cloying. He does what was expected of him. Had he been even partially corrupt and of easy virtue he could have been bribed into owning up about the whereabouts of Billy and ended everything there and then. Also, since Billy soon acquired the much coveted status in his new society and Dhunia being the closest to him, Dhunia never portrayed as taking any advantage of his proximity to Billy. He never seeks any special favour from Billy or even later from the administration and goes on living as before.

Billy Biswas being at the centre of the story, there are just two male characters who play the most important role in his life- Romi and Dhunia. Romi was to Billy before disappearance what Dhunia was to him afterwards. Before the disappearance of Billy Biswas it was Romi who step by step and partially understood what may have been eating the mind of his friend. It was partly due to this understanding of the mind of Billy and partly due to his friendship with Billy that Romi had sympathy for Billy and his adventurous journey after his disappearance. On the other hand, Dhunia had nothing to understand and nor could he be expected to since for him Billy was a man who entered their world of his own choice and before much could be reasoned he was his mahaprasad. Romi understand Billy as a person and as an individual, Dhunia sees him as a helpless soul in flesh and blood who is not responsible for his deeds since he is under the absolute spell of the supernatural. Even when Billy had once rebuked Dhunia he was forgiven on two accounts; one he was his mahaprasad and secondly because he was thought to be under the spell of the witchcraft as 'what gave him [Dhunia] the energy to do the needful [to conceal information about his being there] was not so much the fear of bloodshed as the firm conviction that a person crippled by magic, especially one who was his mahaprasad, had to be defended at all costs' (105).

Of the tribal women in the novel there is only one who is known to us and she is the only one who the reader knows by name and she is Bilasia, the tribal woman Billy married. She was the daughter of the jungle and she was devoid of any superficiality that many in the city are loaded with. When Romi first saw her that is after Billy was shot dead, he admits, "... I was facing not merely a human being but also the embodiment of that primal and invulnerable force that had ruled these hills, perhaps this earth, since time began and that, our proud clairns to the contrary, still lay in wait for us not far from the doorstep of our air conditioned rooms." She was most instrumental in indirectly moulding the already precarious and ambiguous mind of Billy Biswas and she proved to be the ultimate harbour on which Billy decided to embark in his journey, the course of which he knew not more than the others. She did not entice him for one night but had charm enough to 'retain' him for good. Romi had little unease in describing her as, "... that untamed beauty that comes to flower only in our primitive people. It was as though nature were cocking a snook at the Meena Biswases of the world, informing them once again how little it cared for their self- proclaimed superiority. Looking at Bilasia one could well believe that these were the children of kings condemned to exile by those rapacious representatives of civilizations who had ruled the thrones of Delhi and still continued to do so".

Bilasia is shown in a different light than Dhunia. To the very end, having been Billy's wife for ten years and having borne him children, she was still the same -

untamed, ferociously independent, truthful and yet innocent. During the final search for Billy, once his father and wife had come to know about his being alive, Romi comes to Billy's house where he meets his wife Bilasia and their children. Bilasia comes across to the District collector with pride, dignity and straightforwardness.

'I am the collector of the district."

'What do you want?'

'I am old friend of your husband.'

'Where you come from, my husband has no friend."

'That is not so. You are mistaken'

'What do you want?'

'I want to see your husband immediately.'

Her eyes narrowed.

"What for?

'It is for his own good.'

'What for do you want to see him? I know you have come to take him away.

'That is not true.'

'Here, put your hand on my son's head and say you will not take him away' (162-136).

This conversation is proof enough to show how Bilasia stood her ground in the presence of the government officials and the police. All her concentration was focused on the safety of her husband only because she was not frightened but also because she was plain at heart. She was sure and convinced that she had not committed any sin. He had come from a world that was too crafty and powerful and could claim him anytime and even drag him away if possible She did what she thought of as her duty and that was safety and proection of her husband at any cost. It was this duty that she performed with all her might and wisdom even though, in the process, she was vulnerable and helpless.

Bilasia is the central woman character in the novel. Another woman who comes closest to Bilasia in nature, is Tuula, a Swedish woman Billy had met in the United States. Billy admired a quality in Tuula that she always spoke what she thought and thought what she spoke. More than what appealed the most to Billy was Tuula's lack of love for money. Billy once mentioned to Romi, "She was the first person I met for whom money had no value. Since coming here, I have met several others- my present wife [Bilasia], for example- but she was the first" (162). They both were common in their instincts and thinking towards life. It is this serenity of nature and truthfulness that commands the reader's respect. Two other women in the novel are Meena and Rima. Meena was the first wife of Billy and technically his only wife. Billy saw her as irreconcilable and a product of the soulless modern civilisation. Rima was a young girl who was passionately in love with Billy and dies in a car accident.

Bilasia and Rima are both independent and self-determined. They both help Billy in their own way Rima's affair with Billy helped him to wake up and respond to what had been calling him for years (at least that is how he put it) and give him a new direction. His adulterous experience with Rima in Bombay brought him to the last point of his journey of the first half and it was his experience with Bilaisa that led him into the next one. Billy recalls the aftermath of his first experience had been severe enough to cut from the thirty years of his past, but not strong or coherent enough to provide him the basic of a new one. Billy claims to Romi, "I was afraid that after all this upheaval I may still not have found the place where I really wanted to be. What helped me more than anything else was Bilasia. Girls like Bilasia are a whole lot more independent than our own girls, you know that" (106-107)?

What remains to be desired is that more decisive role could have been played by the tribals and their characters could have been elaborated (which does not mean glorified). Any attempt to reason this out by stating that such undermining of tribal characters is nothing but a reflection of 'reality' would not suffice for this is the result of the identity of the tribal that has been constructed in the mind of the other. Almost half the space in the novel is occupied by the tribal world and even then there are merely two characters who are known, no matter how little. It never struck the author that the entire tribal world, represented through just two characters, was serving the protagonist Billy Biswas and his destiny.

The greatest difference between Arun Joshi's The Strange Case of Billy Biswas and Gita Mehta's A River Sutra is that whereas the central concern of the former is Billy Biswas and his 'strange case' that found manifestation in the tribal world, in the latter it is the river Narmada, fables and practices around it and some tribal characters who are strewn around the story line. The latter has no linear plot but episodes which have nothing in common, but the holy purifying river

Narmada, the Narmada Guest House to a lesser extent. A one-time powerful bureaucrat retires into self exile as the manager of the Narmada Guest House. The rest of the novel deals with tales of visiting pilgrims and others who have something or the other, directly or indirectly to do with the river.

The first description of the tribals in the novel is a commonplace mention by the narrator-

On my return in two hours I will be greeted on this path by sturdy tribal women from the nearby village of Vano collecting fuelwood for their cooking. Our bungalow guards, hired from Vano village, enjoy a reputation for fierceness as descendants of the tribal races that held the Aryan invasion of India at bay for centuries in these hills. Indeed, the Vano Village deity is a stone image of a half-woman with the full breasts of fertility symbol but the torso of a coiled snake, because the tribal believe they once ruled a great snake kingdom unit they were defeated by the gods of the Aryans. Saved by annihilation only by a divine personification of the Narmada River, the grateful tribals conferred on the river the gift of annulling the effects of snake bite, and I have often heard pilgrims who have never met a tribal reciting the invocation.

Salutation in the morning and at night to thee, O Narmada! Defend me from the serpent's poison.

The Vano villagers also believe their goddess cures madness, liberating those who are possessed.

There are many stories revolving around the river Narmada and the Narmada Guest House. However, the only story that concerns or involves the tribals is that of Nitin Bose, the young man who had been the executive of a tea company in Calcutta. He came to the Narmada Guest House to cure himself of the 'possession' by a spirit.

He believed to have been possessed by a spirit while he was with a tribal woman called Rima while he was working as the manager of a tea estate in the interior.

In this novel the tribals play a role that is ordinarily decorative. They do not have as much to do, or seem to do as in Arun Joshi's *The Strange Case of Billy Biswas*. Tribals in Gita Mehta's *A River Sutra* play minor roles at two places. One in the life of the manager of the Narmada Guest House and more intensely in the life of Nitin Bose. Even in the latter's case the role is necessarily secondary, though with more just portrayal, the role of the tribals, especially the woman Rima could have been more detailed and just. Instead the role of the tribals is romanticised, mystified and at times even trivialised.

To start with, it is important to know what role is played by the tribals in the life of the manager of the Narmada Gust house, who had been a bureaucrat. As the bureaucrat was returning from Tariq Mia, the Mulla of a nearby mosque, after listening to the depressing story of the murder of the young singer Imrat, he met a few tribal women on the way. He narrator describes how he saw their saris sloding from their shoulders, baring their waists and the curve of their full breast to his view as they stacked bundles of wood onto the small donkeys grazing under the trees. He remarks thar their sturdy bodies, their catlike faces with the triangular tattoo marks offered high greetings with uncharacteristic warmth and that they nudged each other in surprise on seeing him.

"The sahib finds your face pretty today, Rano."

"It must be the season. Spring rouses even old tigers from their rest."

"It's true. Don't you see a prowl to the Sahib's walk this morning?"

The former bureaucrat observes how their provocative laughter followed him down the gentle incline of the path as he heard them say, "Be careful not to walk alone, sisters. The mango trees are in bloom. Kama must be sharpening his arrows of blossoms and stringing his bow with bees, sisters. Take care he does not lure us to seduction".

This role played by these women working on the wayside field is typical of the overall role assigned to the tribal fairer sex. While the men are supposed to be submissive, and when they are not, they are criminal and the women are lusty seductresses who are of easy virtue and ever ready to part with their honour. They have no other role to play other than being the objects of eroticism and the dialogues attributed to them show that they are always pre-occupied with sensual pleasures. The bureaucrat then adds- "Grateful to the laughing women for lifting my gloom, I returned to wave at them but they had disappeared and only the green canopy of the jungle rustled over the hill".

Taking up the last observation made by the old bureaucrat, it can be rightly said that the two things associated with tribal characters, by and large, in Indian fiction in English are their role in 'lifting the gloom' of the first main non-tribal characters, ie, they play secondary role which is used to highlight the main developments in the life of the protagonist or the other main characters. About their 'disappearance" it can only be said that these characters are considered to be too unimportant and inconsequential to be drawn to any meaningful conclusion. Once their whatever supportive role is over they are made to 'disappear' without leaving any memorable trace behind for others to remember or locate. The whole understanding of the tribal world is summed up towards the end of chapter five, "What a brilliant mind be enough to protect the young man from the dark forces of the jungle, from the tribal worship of that desire which even their conquerors had acknowledged to be invincible, describing it as the first born seed of the mind?"

Nitin Bose, the young executive had been, before coming to the Narmade Guest House, a manager of the tea garden where for miles one couldn't find any people and most of the laborers were tribals, and especially women The notions that most executives had about these wonen were-

"Real women who will do anything to please a man."

"And what sexual appetites. It's all they think about."

"I couldn't touch those hideous creatures unless I was stinking drunk."

"I bet they smell like hell, your real women."

Then begins the story of how this manager from Calcutta was seduced by this mysterious women called Rima who joined him only at nights, indulging in love-making, left in the mornings. Nitin Bose was enchanted by all this romantic and magical association. This goes on for long. Nitin Bose meanwhile got a call from Calcutta to attend a board meeting. He tells Rima about it. The last time Rima visited him at night, she told him that her husband was away at Agartala and worked as a coolie. That night Nitin saw her clearly. The spell broke and he found her ugly and couldn't stand that he had been involved with a coolie's wife. After coming back from Calcutta he was misled into the forest on a full moon night by his name being called out by Rima. That night he was possessed by the spirit that guaranteed Rima that Nitin would never leave her. This is where the role of Rima ends. Now Nitin comes to the Narmada Guest House to visit a tribal shrine where he could be cured of his madness. He also wrote a paper on tribal customs. He was then taken to be cured at the shrine of the tribal goddess on the banks of Narmada.

Once again the role of the tribals in the novel is questionable. Rima plays an important role in determining the course of life of Nitin Bose. But we are told of her only as a seductress and an enchanting women about whom we know nothing except that she had inexhaustible sexual appetite. She is depicted as magical and mysterious. We are told nothing about their lives, problems and other issues concerning their very existence. They are made to look like unreal and lusty characters straight out of the fantasy world. This substantiates our argument that these writers are not firmly and fully grounded in the tribal reality and this outsider's point of view is certainly not a convincing one about the reality of the tribal world.

Notes:

1. Arundhati Roy's reaction to Ramchandra Guha's biography of Verrier Elwin encapsulates a problematic tendency in writing on the issues related to the tribals, which is that of condescension towards them. It is a distancing attitude. The title of Guha's book thus earned Roy's ire: 'And the title of his book! Savaging the Civilized Verrier Elwin, His Tribals, and India His Tribals! His tribals? For Heaven's sake! Did he own then? Did he buy them?? (Roy 7) This observation by Arundhati Roy not only underlines but also protests against the patronization of the tribals in India, be it in writing of fiction or, as in this case, a biography Guha's biography of Verrier Elwin may not be indulging in such patronization on the whole but the title of the book is not much further from it.

Works Cited:

Alexander, S. and Indra Bhatt, Arun Joshi's Fiction: A Critique, New Delhi: Creative Books, 2001. Print.
Bhatnagar, M. K., ed. The Novels of Arun Joshi: A Critical Study, New Delhi: Atlantic Publishers, 2001. Print.

Chakrabarty, Shirshendu. Introduction. The Chieftan's Daughter: Durgeshnandini. 1865. By Bankim Chandra Chattopadhyay. Trans. Arunava Sinha. New Delhi: Random House, 2010. Print.

Chattopadhyay, Bankim Chandra. The Chieftan's Daughter: Durgeshnandini, 1865, Trans. Arunava Sinha. New Delhi: Random House, 2010. Print

Dharwadkar, Vinay. "English in India and Indian Literature in English: The Early History, 1579-1834" (93-119). Comparative Literature Studies. Vol. 39, November 2, 2002. Pennyslyvania: Pennyslyvania State UP. Google Book Search Web. 23 June 2010.

Dhawan, R. K. The Fictional World of Arun Joshi. New Delhi: Classical Publishig Company, 1986. Print.

Fisher, Michael, H. The First Indian Author in English (Dean Muhomed 1759-1851) in India, Ireland and England. New Delhi: OUP, 2000. Google Book Search, Web. 23 June 2010.

_ _ _. The Travels of Dean Mahomet: An Eighteenth Century Journey Through India, Berkely: University of California, 1997. Google Book Search. Web. 23 June 2010.

Furer- Haimendorf, C. von. "The Tribal Problem in All-India Perspective." Tribes of India The Struggle for Survival. New Delhi: OUP, 1982. Print.

Guha, Ramchandra, India After Gandhi: The History of the World's Largest Democracy. London: Picador, 1997. Print.

_ _ _. Savaging the Civilized: Verrier Elwin, His Tribals, and India. Chicago: Chicago UP, 1999. Print.

Ghosh, Amitav. Sea of Poppies. New Delhi: Penguin, 2008. Print

Joshi, Arun. The Strange Case of Billy Biswas. New Delhi. Orient, 1971. Print. Khair, Tabish. "In the Shadow of the Empire". India Today: 11 June 2012. Print.

Mukherjee, Meenakshi. The Perishable Empire: Essays on Indian Writing in English. New Delhi: OUP, 2000. Print.

Patil, Mallikarjun. "Arun Joshi's Fictional Forte." The Novels of Arun Joshi: A Critical Study. Ed. M.K. Bhatnagar. New Delhi: Atlantic Publishers, 2001. Print.

Roy, Arundhati. The Shape of the Beast: Conversation with Arundhati Roy. New Delhi: Penguin, 2008.

Roy, Nilanjana S. "In Midnight's Shadow" Business Standard 15 July 2008. Print.

Singh, Khushwant. "Opium Eaters." Hindustan Times, 08 June, 2008. Print.

Singh, Pankaj K., ed. The Politics Of Literary Theory and Representation: Writing on Activism and Aesthetics. New Delhi: Manohar Publications, 2003. Print.

Spivak, Gayatri Chakravarty. "A Literary Representation of the Subaltern: Mahasweta Devi's 'Standayini'." Indian Literary Criticism Theory and Interpretation. Ed. G. N. Devy New Delhi: Orient Longman, 2002. Print.

Vachaspati, D. The Fictional Art of Arun Joshi An Existential Perspective. New Delhi: Atlantic Publishers, 2004. Print.

Wright, Gillian. "Her Last Hurrah: Book Review of Kamala Markandaya's Bombay Tiger". India Today, 25 February 2008. Print.

Chapter - 6

Conclusion

Adibhoomi is indeed a novel, but based on truth. Reality and imagination have been assimilated here into one whole. Human being's hope and imagination give birth to a dream- and a civilization is born of that dream. Out of that dream and imagination is born the history of that civilization, and through that history is born the novel. The novel in turn breeds new dreams, new history.

(Pratibha Ray's Introduction to *Adibhoomi*)

This study set out to examine representation of the tribal Indian subjectivities at two levels; one the theory of representation in itself and the repercussions of representation, and secondly the manner in which the tribal population of India is represented in the novels that had been taken up for the purpose of study. Since the study did not involve any project to study the practical aspects of the lives of the tribals and focused only on the representation, particularly in selected novels, it, however, intends to be useful in reflecting upon some real-life issues, such as understanding the, '...association between representation and reality' (Stephens 93).

The discussion in the thesis demonstrates sensitivity towards a representation of a section of society in a popular medium such as fiction. Of the five authors whose selected novels were chosen for this study, four belonged to regional Indian languages, Oriya, Marathi and Bengali.

In The Continent of Circe (1965), Nirad C. Chaudhary writes: "In an industrialized India the destruction of the aboriginal's life is as inevitable as the submergence of the Egyptian temples caused by the dams of the Nile.... As things are going, there can be no grandeur in the primitive's end. It will not be even simple extinction, which is not the worst of human destinies. It is to be feared that the aboriginal's last act will be squalid, instead of being tragic What will be seen with most regret will be, not his disappearance, but his enslavement and degradation" (Furer- Haimendorf 1982: 313)

Having quoted Chaudhary Furer-Haimendorf's notes:

Fifteen years ago Nirad Chaudhary, the provocative analyst of the Indian social scene, published this gloomy forecast, and the readers...may well agree that the dice are heavily loaded against the likelihood of an unclouded future for the 40 million Indian aboriginals [as per 1980 census)....However, the choice of the road which any tribal society will take is hardly ever left to the tribesmen themselves but is imposed on them by external circumstances outside their own control (313).

These observations made above have come closer to the gloomy reality they may have so painfully predicted. In the present time, protests by tribal communities are being held in most parts of India. The greatest reason of confrontation is land, and therefore, forests. Uprooting tribal communities from their land, most of whom have no documents to their ownership, with little compensation, has marred their destiny and rendered them vulnerable.

Such encounters of the tribals in the modern period remind the reader instantly of Birsa Munda and his struggle against the restrictions imposed by the British government upon the use of forests. It goes to Mahashweta Devi's credit for being acutely sensitive to the phenomenon of Birsa Munda and his movement which had the only objective of restoring the use of forest lands to people living in the forests. To learn that even in modern independent India, the tribal population shall have to cope with the same everyday brutality, is nothing less than disheartening.

It is, therefore, understood that 'representation' of the tribal communities [for that matter of any community or person or nation] is a sensitive matter, that of the tribal communities more so since they have been more vulnerable to exploitation and condemnation. Unfair representation, done intentionally or otherwise, breeds doubt and ill feelings in the minds of the readers or the consumers of the 'portraya!'; through literature, journalism, cinema, theatre or television, and therefore leads to contemptuous thinking towards them, which makes it simpler for the predators to justify any sort of behavior towards them.

As has been pointed out earlier in the thesis, loose usage of the word "tribal" should be avoided. Writers and commentators in the west have shown a greater susceptibility towards this practice. Writing about soccer nationalism in Europe, lan Buruma associates 'tribal feelings' with 'collective effort, the team colours, the speed and physical aggression' (2008). The characteristics recognised as 'tribal' need not necessarily be associated with it for these are found abundantly in all human societies.

One may question Buruma's first-hand knowledge of having experienced such behavior among the tribal communities. Of course, Buruma's statements have come not from any such experience but from the unconscious state of mind where such interpretations and information have been stored, which in itself is a result of having read or watched other peoples' representations, which too may not have been based on first-hand experience or may have been biased due to reasons; colonial, political, religious or any other, in nature. It may not inflict pain and humiliation in many parts of the world where it is an archaic concept but can wreck considerable damage in many other parts of the world, particularly India, where almost one hundred million people are constitutionally recognised as 'scheduled tribes' and have been at the receiving end of the national development'.

The image of the tribals in fiction and films is very important for the literary and social historians mainly for two reasons-(1) these two mediums in recent times have come up as the most effective, popular and powerful mediums of representations, and (2) the images of subjects represented in these artifacts are largely determined by the social reality and also, have an impact on that reality. The ancient epics and other narratives reiterate these claims. The tribal characters in the Ramayana and the Mahabharata and the Sanskrit literary texts are considered representative of the times.

The tribal situation in India underwent a sea change during British rule when the introduction of a series of Forest acts intended to serve the imperialist interests, mainly economic, disturbed the tribals in terms of their forest rights. The Forest Acts in the post-independent India were changed to some extent but there was not much change in the tribal situation. Only the agents and forces of exploitation had a new name and a new face. The forest wealth is still the target of the 'civilised world and the process of tribal exploitation has graduated to different stages dispossessing the tribals from the forests on one pretext of the other.

The enormous power wielded by the forest guard in Gopinath Mohanty's Paraja is a classic example of how the petty official of the forest department wrecks havoc on a fairly happy and a prosperous family of Sukru Jani. Till then the family had been living the life of reasonable prosperity within the bounds of subsistence agriculture, by practicising shifting agriculture. The fortunes of the family are turned up side down when Sukru Jani refuses to offer his daughter to the demands of the forest guard who had seen the young one bathing at a river. The novel narrates the moving tale of a family who begin by a quiet refusal to part with their honour and suffer humiliation and expoitation in the process and ends with extreme violence on the part of the hapiess tribals who knew no other way of breaking the vicious circle of repeated humiliation, subjugation and an imminent collapse of their lives under the oppression of the government officials and the local moneylender.

As mentioned earher in the discussion the study comes under the umbrella term of subaltern studies and it aims to contest and subvert the literary stereotypes of the tribal. Conrad's Heart of Darkness for instance, typifies the distorted image of the African and Africa as a dark and gloomy continent, and now the African literary, critical and theoretical discourse challenges that biased Eurocentric version of Africa. On similar lines, it is imperative to break the old stereotypes of the tribal in literature and films and create the new identities that are representational in spirit. Therefore, it becomes imperative to interrogate the identity or representation of the tribal in fiction and films, the two most recent genres of representation in the modern literary canon and reconstruct it. In 1985 Gayatri Spivak threw a challenge, asking Can the Subaltern speak?' (Leela Gandhi 1). By subaltern, Spivak meant the oppressed subjects, the people 'of inferior rank', the members of Antonio Gramsci's 'subaltern classes whose voices, history and experiences had been largely missing from the dominant literary and social canon in the South Asian Studies and to promote a systematic and informed discussion of subaltern themes in the field of South Asian Studies in terms of class, caste, age, gender or in any other way.

Colonialism and imperialism are institutionalised systems of power and control. The subaltern studies discourse intends to focus upon the voices of the people of Antonio Gramsci's people of inferior rank. The reclamation and subsequent relocation of the subaltern voices in the dominant canon is the agenda of the subaltern discourse. The power of colonial discourse was that it created whole new meanings instantaneously but that it shifted old meanings slowly, sometimes imperceptively through the colonial control of a whole range of institutions. Caste, tribe, religion are some of the key institutions that have acquired some of the new meanings in the colonial estate.

The field and scope of subaltern studies is not limited to literature but it surpasses many areas in order to present (or represent) a coherent whole by bringing in its compass fields such as Politics, Geography, Media, Sociology and Anthropology. It is an effort to reconstruct the reality of the past and to lend clearef interpretation of not just the historical processes but also the present. The effort goes not just to represent the deprived sections of the society and the marginalized cities, cultures and nations vis-a-vis their masters but also lends a voice to the further peripherised groups within a dominated or a dominating social, political, economic and cultural system "In other words, 'subaltern studies' defined itself as an attempt to allow the 'people' finally to speak within the jealous pages of elitist historiography and, in so doing, to speak for, or to sound the muted voices of, the truly oppressed (Gandhi 2).

At the centre stage of this entire academic activity is the polemics of representation' of one by the other. This 'representation' may be in literature, cultural or political hierarchy. During a period of domination, the subjugated is represented 'suitabley' by the one that claims to be the master. This is so, in order to achieve political goals through the sense of sustained superiority over the dominated one. The 'complex notion of subalternity is pertinent to any academic enterprise which concerns itself with historically determined relationships of dominance and subordination. Yet it is postcolonial studies which have responded with the greatest enthusiasm to Spivak's 'Can the subaltern speak?' paradigm. Utterly unanswerable, half-serious and half-parodic, this question circulates around the self-conscious scene of postcolonial text, theory, conferences and conversations (2)

The shift in the 'representations of the subaltern classes has led to various impartial players to join the field and enable them to 'speak up' or to 'speak for them" more reasonably, without bias and without any apparent motive (social, political or cultural). The tribal population in recent years has caught the attention of social activists, writers and artists alike. Mahasweta Devi, Arundhati Roy, Pratibha Ray, Amitav Ghosh, Gopinath Mohanty and Ramachandra Guha are some of the prominent Indian writers whose works, fictional as well as non-fictional, are firmly foregrounded in the tribal reality. Their fiction represents and translates the tribal reality in literature. Mahasweta Devi, for instance, is a powerful writer-cum-social activist, who addresses the various issues and dimensions of the tribal reality in he stories in terms of gender and politics of power.

Draupadi is one of Mahashweta Devi's most famous stories located among the tribals in Bengal. She is a rebel hunted down by the government agencies in the form of police and the army officials the Senanayak Despite the coercive powers employed by the government by means of kidnapping, murder and rape, the female protagonist emerges as the 'victor. Dropdi's silence is suggestive of the most powerful mode of the 'subaltern speak. Spivak states, "When we speak for ourselves, we urge with conviction: the personal is also political. For the rest of the world's women, the sense of whose personal micrology is difficult (though not impossible) for us to acquire, we fall back on a colonialist theory of most efficient information retrieval. We will not be able to speak to the women out there if we depend completely on conferences and anthologies by Western-trained informants" (382).

Deprived of food, water and subjected to physical abuse, she faces her abusers with the stark nakedness of her body. Profusely bleeding, her mortal fortitude and undaunted spirit remind the readers of Hemingway's heroes, defeated in body but not in mind and spirit, Santiago in *The Old Man And The Sea* specifically.

There are many such instances of tribal action in their moments of glory but the English fiction writers have, however, promoted the stereotypes of docile, quiet, unthinking and unthinkable tribals that we have discussed in the preceding chapter during the discussion of *The Strange Case of Billy Biswas* and Gita Mehta's *A River Sutra*. It may be debated as to what extent the English language is responsible for the Indian writers in English to feel obliged to touch the issue of the tribals from a safe distance. It is possible that the language or the assumed readership play an important role in determining the role or the portrayal of the tribal characters in the novels.

As a welcome point of departure, the new art cinema, on the contrary, has reflected on the nuances of tribal life and portrayed tribals in new roles and situations. One representative cinematic image the spectators would prefer to remember is of a boy shattering the windowpane of the exploiter landlord in the film Ankur. The symbolic resistance no doubt comes from a small boy but is very meaningful and pregnant with futuristic meaning. These two examples from literature and films are substantive of the importance fiction and films have in improving our understanding of the subject.

The tribal question is not without its own share of dilemma involving various issues of identity and self. Who are the indigenous people of the land? Who are the 'natives of the peninsula? Over the years the tribals, in addition to having been pushed into oblivion (even geographically) have also been 'mixing' with the 'non-tribal population. Many sections of the Indian Society who were declared as the 'Scheduled Tribes do not share many characteristics with the mainstream tribal population and several such 'genuine' and 'authentic sections of the tribal society find themselves out of the constitutional tribal circle. "In the politics of identifying authentic natives several strands of the word 'identification' are at stake. How do we identify the native? How do we identify with her? How do we construct the native's identity? What processes of identification are involved?" (Chow 123).

In a civilised society, literature is a serious medium of expression and communication. It serves the purpose of enlightening the society about truth that is prevalent in the society. Literature about a society thus becomes its cultural representation. We understand the fabric, the ethos and the objectives of our earlier societies through our cpics, narratives and other literary genres poetry and drama have been written from time to time. One can not undermine the importance of literature during the centuries of empire as it was the written word that served as the "wheels of the empire', therefore, after the demise of the empire, in addition to political self-determination, it is the rewriting and the reinterpretation of literary texts that is given due importance.

Literature on the tribal society is broadly of two types - One that romanticises their reality to suit the interests and wishes of the readers. Secondly, the one that deals with the real portrayal of their subjectivity even if it is, sometimes, at the cost of the absence of the dramatic and the creative elements that add colour and life to fiction.

It is the second type of contemporary Indian literature such as the regional Bengali, Oriya, Hindi, Assamese etc. that was selected for this study. The picture that comes across of the tribal world in these novels is far from pleasing. It is in fact a very disturbing portrayal/representation of reality. These writers have depicted the Socio- Economic reality of our tribal world that is not easy to evade. Pratibha Ray's *Adibhoomi* oscillates between the twin possibilities of changing and developing the tribal population by adopting the strategies of the mainstream society. However, the dismal results are for everyone to see. The development that had been anticipated does not show in real terms since the projects are carried out without the willing participation of the supposed beneficiaries. The outside world, which considers itself 'civilised' enough and thus enforces its way of living and development of a people who feel no need for it. In turn, the bondas of Koraput had their language enriched by vocabulary such as orphan, illegal, outcaste, fallen woman, homeless and mad (*Adibhoomi* 438). The novel also narrates an incident when no one raised a hand when the development officer called to identify the poor among the bondas. The unanimous reply was that there was no poor or rich among the bondas as each looked after the other's well being. The development process, however, divided them into two categories- rich and poor- by bribing some to declare themselves to be poor and live in the newly built houses built under the Indira Awas Yojana, in order to impress the visiting officials (*Adibhoomi 392*).

Pratibha Ray comments on the role of the development process in the bondage. When she visited the habitation of the Bonds to carry out research on *The Impact of Education on the Criminal Tendencies of the Bondas from 1985 to 1993* - she found that there had been just eight primary schools since 1960, and all existed only on paper and the teachers received their salaries at home. Also, those who are the responsible agents are full of contempt and indifference and quick to shed crocodile tears.

The tribal population has indeed been pushed to the brink of rebellion, even if it is gathering momentum silently. Decades of negligence and corruption (in the various government schemes) by the Indian state bring out the worst in them when sometimes they vent their feelings through violence. A Srinivas writes in an article, "Naxalites Today":

> *It is hardly surprising that Naxal influence is strongest in tribal India. Tribals, more than any other oppressed category, have got nothing out of the Indian state, before or after globalization. The Indian state has always taken land alienation of tribals for granted, as one of the consequences of 'progress' that must be put up with. Owing to a skewed pattern of land distribution, tribals and dalits are at the receiving end of the land owning castes. In addition, a contractor- politician nexus controls the wealth of the forests and pushes tribals to the margins. A repressive state apparatus, represented by the police and the laws they use to their advantage, helps keep this exploitative system going.*

With the opening up of the Indian economy to trade and investment, not only by the Indian industrialists and business houses but the multinationals as well as the entry of mining companies in Orissa and Chattisgarh poses a threat to the livelihood of tribals and their way of life. Naxalites are among those though not the only one - who are with the tribals in this context. Even as their adherence to violence cannot be condoned, it is now worse than the violence of the state and oppressive force in the region.

Ramachandra Guha, the author of *India After Gandhi*, reveals the bleak tribal reality in the following terms, "The group that has been most shafted by Indian democracy is tribals.1 The obvious comparison is with Dalits and Muslims. The latter are represented in the cabinet. You've had presidents and judges. Political parties at least pay lip service to the ideals and aspirations of Dalits and Muslims, but not so tribals" (2007).

The tribal population is rapidly being aliented from their natural resources such as forests and their cultivation fields. Most of their activities are being controlled by state regulations. It may be the case of the honey collectors of Sunderbans who threaten to boycott election since their source of livelihood is being snatched away by the state or the refugees from the site of a hydel-project, the tribal everywhere is living in a no-man's land. There is nowhere where they have legitimate claim to the soil.

The notification of Scheduled Tribes and Traditional Forest Dwellers (Recognition of Forest Rights) Act 2006 led to a debate of a very different kind: Tigers vs Tribals (Anant Sudarshan, 2008). The forest legislation throughout the British era, according to Sudarshan, including the 1927 Indian Forest Act, was 'premised upon a treatment of India's forests as a source of revenue', and saw 'their habitants as an inconvenience to be removed. Thus the 2006 Act led conservationists to suspect that the tribals' intrusion into the forests would lead to the extinction of the tigers. Independent India's insensitivity towards the rights of tribals and their intimacy with and dependence upon the natural world around them is demonstrated by the fact that not till 1988 did the government of India wake to recognise this reality and that too was lost due to the non-implementation of the Indian Forest Policy which was passed in the same year. It was as a result of such indifference that, "With no rights over land declared as forest, today, over 62 percent of the adivasi people are completely landless" (Sudarshan 2008). The solution, that Sudarshan suggests is the middle path, which could be the only path left to tread is, "...we need to acknowledge that the debate that is necessary is not whether we should provide rights to people, but rather how we can do so and still protect our natural heritage".

Ekta Parishad, a Gandhian organization has been mobilizing the landless since1999. In October 2007 the Parishad organized Janadesh 2007, a padayatra of 25,000 landless people from Gwalior to New Delhi, to highlight the issues of livelihood. Its Presidentg P.V. Rajagopal was interviewed:

Q. Your slogan is- 'land for landless'. How do you see the legislation that recognises the right of tribals over forest land?

Ans. If you don't settle the claims of tribal communities, you won't be able to protect the forest. When an adivasi raises a crop and the forest authorities raze it, he doesn't leave the forest to migrate to the city. He only moves to another patch of land. Tribal communities should be helped to shift from *jhum* cultivation to settled agriculture. The state took away their forests. Return that so they live as hunters or food gatherers or allow them to be farmers. Now, don't ask adivasi's for proof to substantiate their claim over land. Go by oral testimonies. If they don't have papers like the *jurmana* receipt that is because the state has been corrupt.'

In another question about rural poverty and employment the president of the Parishad said, "...the boom sector in employment is that of the security guards People who have sold land are employed by the new owner to guard that land there is migration among tribals in Madhya Pradesh, Chhattisgarh and Jharkhand. Tribals have always resisted migration to urban areas. That has changed due to mining, etc. Agricultural land is now either being converted into real estate or is contracted by companies. For every hundred factory jobs, thousand opportunities of independent, self-employment are destroyed".

So long as the issues of the tribals are not dealt with in a just manner the literature representing them shall continue to give a bleak picture of an equally depressing reality. The real point is to treat the tribals as fellow human beings who are equal and not just the ones who pay a heavy price for the development and prosperity of the rest and prosperity of the rest of India. The point is also to give credit to their real achievements. The revolt of 1857 is given the title of the First War of Independence. As Ramanika Gupta points out that this was a war fought by the monarchs in order to retain their kingdoms from being annexed by the British Empire. The real wars against the Raj began much earlier in the second half of the eighteenth century and those prolonged battles were not just initiated but sustained by the tribal heroes and their people.

Serious literature about tribals, in addition to the encouragement and recognition it has received, needs more endorsement at national and international level so that more aspects of tribal reality are brought to the notice of a wider readership and general public. The challenges that we confront today are as to how to integrate the so called tribal societies into the manifold mainstream society. Unlike earlier times when the tribal societies were brought into the mainstream society by incorporating them into the caste system and when most of them found a place at the bottom of the caste hierarchy, so called tribes are today armed with democracy. It would still be a matter of debate to what extent democracy has equipped the deprived masses to fight for themselves. As has been mentioned earlier in the thesis, Ramchandra Guha, however, would rather have something very contrary to say:

> *These [the problems of Dalits, Muslims, female foeticide, khap panchayat) are real problems, which must be discussed, and addressed. But so must the situation of the adivasis who lose their lands to mines and dams, the adivasis deprived of access to schools and hospitals, the adivasis who are ignored by the media and the political parties, the adivasis who are massively under-represented in the professional classes and in the upper reaches of the bureaucracy, the adivasis subject to violence by State and insurgent alike. The adivasis are the most vulnerable, the most victimised of Indians. (2011).*

Literature and life have existed together, and apart from literature reflecting life, it also has a lasting impact upon the latter. It is this sensitivity between the two that necessitates a study of this nature. This study is a sort of feedback or a reaction from life towards literature that claims to represent it. The sincerity of this reaction legitimises the important role that the representation of people of certain class, caste, group or a section plays since such representation has a direct bearing upon not just the perception that society in general shall possess of them but upon their very lives

Notes:

1. In the same article - It's Harmless Flag Flying, Buruma continues, "Just as killing continues to be celebrated in ritualized form in Spanish bull rings, illicit tribal feelings are given full vent in the soccer areans", "The tribal feelings of Germans were considered, for obvious reasons, to be particularly toxic after Hitler's Reich, which is why German flag-waving, until recently, was exercised with a slight air or shame-faced restraint that was entirely absent in surrounding countries and Clubs, too, often used to command tribal loyalty along ethnic or religious lines...."

2. As Aijaz Ahmed has pointed out that in India there seems to be developing a new urban culture, "for whom only the literary document produced in English is a national document. All else is regional, hence minor and forgettable, so that English emerges as one of the Indian languages, which it undoubtedly is, but as the language of literary sophistication and bourgeois civility" (Mukherjee 182).

Works Cited:

Buruma, lan. "It's Harmless Flag Flying: Football Nationalism is on the Wane in Europe." The Times of India. 03 July, 2008. Print.

Chow, Rey. "Where Have All The Natives Gone"? Contemporary Postcolonial Theory. 1996. Ed. Padmini Mongia. New Delhi: OUP, 2004. Print.

Furer- Haimendorf, C. von. "The Tribal Problem in All-India Perspective." Tribes of India: The Struggle for Survival, New Delhi: OUP, 1982. Print.

Gandhi, Leela. Postcolonial Theory: A Critical Introduction. New Delhi: OUP, 1998. Print.

Guha, Ramachandra. Interview. The Times of India. New Delhi: 11 May 2007. Print.

Lost in the Woods. Hindustan Times. 15 August 2011. Print.

Gupta, Ramaanika. Yudharata Aam Aadmi. All India Tribal Issue. New Delhi: Raminika Foundation, 2005. Print.

Rajagopal, P.V. Interview. "Settle the Clauns of the Tribals to Protect Forests". The Times of India. New Delhi: 11 June, 2007. Print.

Srinivas, A. Interview. "Naxalites Today". The Times of India, 11 June 2007. Print. Sudarshan, Anant. So, Are

you for the Tigers or the Tribals? The Indian Express.
09 April 2008. Print.

Bibliography

Primary Sources:

Bhattacharya, B.K. *Mrityunjay*. 1980. Trans. K.P.S Magadh. New Delhi: Bhartiya Jananpith, 2005. Print.

Devi, Mahashweta. *Rudali*. 1993. Trans. Anjum Katyal. Calcutta: Seagull, 1997. Print

Joshi, Arun. *The Strange Case of Billy Biswas*. New Delhi: Orient Paperbacks, 1971. Print.

Mohanty, Gopinath. *Maatimataal*. 1964. Trans. Shankarlal Purohit. New Delhi: Jnanpith, 2001. Print.

Paraja. 1945. Trans. Bikram K. Das. New Delhi: OUP, 1987. Print.

Ray, Pratibha. *Aadibhoomi*. 1993. Trans. Shankarlal Purohit. New Delhi: Jnanpith, 2001. Print.

Yajnaseni. 1995. Trans. Pradip Bhattacharya. New Delhi: Rupa, 2002. Print

Secondary Sources:

Achebe, Chinua. Things Fall Apart. 1958. New York: Anchor Books, 1994, Print.

Alam, Javeed. "Fragmented Culture and Strangulated Existence: Jharkhand's Cultural Encounter with the Modern". Continuity and Change in Tribal Society. Ed Mrinal Miri. Shimla IIAS, 1993. Print.

Alam, Jayanti. Tribal Women's Worker: A Study of Young Migrants. New Delhi: Raj Publications, 2000. Print.

Albrow, Martin. Sociology: The Basics. London: Routledge, 1999. Print.

Alexander, S. and Indra Bhatt. Arun Joshi's Fiction: A Critique. New Delhi: Creative Books, 2001. Print.

Allen, Charles. Kipling Sahib India and the Making of Rudyard Kipling, London: Abacus, 2007. Print. Ahmed, Imtiaz "Caste is Relevant." New Delhi: The Times of India. 11 July 2007. Print.

Amin, Shahid. "Approver's Testimony, Judicial Discourse. The Case of Chauri Chaura" 1987. Subaltern Studies. Ed. Ranajit Guha. 2nd ed. Vol. V. New Delhi: OUP, 1995 Print.

Amin, Shahid, and Dipesh Chakrabarty, eds. Subaltern Studies Writings on South Asian History and Society. 1996. Vol. IX. New Delhi: OUP, 2005. Print.

Amin, Shahid and Gyanedra Pandey. Nimnwarguya Prasang: 1. New Delhi: Rajkamal, 1995. Print.

Aristotle. The Politics Trans.T.A. Sinclair. 1962. London: Penguin, 1992. Print.

Arnold, David, and David Hardıman, eds. Subaltern Studies Essays in Honour of Ranajit Guha. 1994. Vol. VIII. New Delhi: OUP, 2005. Print.

Arnold, David. "Rebellious Hillmen: The Gudem Rampa Risings 1839-1924" Subaltern Studies. Writings on South Asian History and Society. 1982. Ed. Ranajit Guha. Vol. L. New Delhi: Oxford UP, 2005. Print.

Badrinath, Chaturvedi. An Inquiry in the Human Condition. New Delhi: Orient Longman, 2006. Print.

Balfour, Edward G., ed. Enclopedia Asiatica: Comprising Indian Subcontinent eastern and southern Asia: Commercial, Industrial and Scientific. 1858. 3rd ed. Vol 5. New Delhi: Cosmo, 1976. Print. 9 vols.

Basham, A L. The Wonder That Was India. 1967. 3rd. ed. New Delhi: Rupa, 1997. Print.

Bowil, Andrew. Aesthetics and Subjectivity. From Kant to Nietzsche. Manchester: Manchester UP, 1990. Google Book Search. Web. 20 December 2010.

Beverly, John. Subalternity and Representation: Arguments in Cultural Theory. Durham: Duke University Press, 1999. Google Book Search. Web.

Bhattacharya, B.K. Marityunjaya, 1998. Trans. K.P.S. Magadh. New Delhi: Bhartiya Jnanpith, 2005. Print.

Bhatnagar, M. K., ed. The Novels of Arun Joshi: A Critical Study. New Delhi: Atlantic Publishers, 2001. Print.

Bochmer, Elleke. Colonial and Postcolonial Literature. 1995. New Delhi: Oxford U P, 2006. Print.

Behura, N.K., and N. Panigrahi. Tribals and the Indian Constitution. New Delhi: Ramat Publication, 2006. Print.

Betts, Raymond F. Decolonization. London: Routledge, 1998. Print.

Bhadra, Gautam, Gyan Prakash, and Susic Tharu, eds. Subaltern Studies: Writigs On South Asian History and Society 1999, Vol. X. New Delhi: OUP, 2005. Print.

Bhatnagar, Manmohan K. Indian Writing in English. Vol. I-V. New Delhi: Atlantive Publishers, 2001. Print.

Brown, Radchiffe, and Daryil Rorde, eds. African Systems of Kinship and Marriage. 1950. London. KPI and Internaional African Institute, 1987. Print.

Bunsha, Dionee "Festival of Fear" New Delhi: Frontline, 10 March 2006. Print.

Carr, EH. What is History. 1961. Victoria Penguin, 2008. Print.

Cederlof, Gunnel, and Sivarama Krishna, K., eds. Ecological Nationalisms: Nature, Livelihoods, and Identities in South Asia. New Delhi: Permanent Black, 2005. Print.

Chakravarty, K.K., G.V. Davis, and G. N. Devy, eds. Indigeneity: Culture and Representation Proceedings of the 2008 Conference on Indigenous Langages, Culture and Society Vol.1. New Delhi: Orient Black Swam, 2009. Print.

Chakrabarty, Monotosh, and Sourav Sanyal. "Sunderbans Honey Collectors To Boycott Election". New Delhi: The Times of India. 10 April, 2006, Print.

Chakrabarty, Shirshendu. Introduction. The Chieftan's Daughter: Durgeshnandini 1865. By Bankim Chandra Chattopadhyay. Trans. Arunava Sinha. New Delhi: Random House, 2010. Print.

Chattopadhyay, Bankim Chandra. The Chieftan's Daughter Durgeshnandini. 1865. Trans. Arunava Sinha. New Delhi: Random House, 2010 Print

Chanda, Nayan. Bound Together How Traders, Preachers, Adventurers, and Warriors Shaped Globalization. Penguin, 2007. Print.

Chandra, Bipan. India After Independence New Delhi: Penguin, 2007. Print.

Chatterjee, Partha, and Pradeep Jeganathan, eds. Subaltern Studies. Community Gender and Violence, Vol. XI. 2000 New Delhi Permanent Black, 2009. Print.

Chatterjee, Partha, and Gyanendra Pandey, eds Subaltern Studies Writings on South Asian History and Society. Vol. VII. 1992 New Delhi Oxford UP, 2005. Print.

Chatterjee, Roma. "The Nationalist Sociology of Benoy Kumar Sarkar" (106-131). Anthropology in the East. Founders of Indian Sociology and Anthropology. Eds Patricia Uberoi, Nandini Sunder and Satish Deshpande. Ranikhet: Permanent Black, 2007. Print.

Chaturvedi, Vinayak. Peasant Parts History. Politics and Nationalism in Gujarat. 2007 Ranikhat: Permanent Black, 2008. Print.

Chaudhary, Damina. Tribal Frils: Aspirations, Achievements and Frustrations. Jaipur Pointer Publishers, 2000 Print.

Chomsky, Noam. The Essential Chomsky. Ed. Anthony Arnove. New Delhi Penguin, 2008. Print.

Chow, Rey. "Where Have All The Natives Gone"? Contemporary Postcolonial Theory. 1996. Ed. Padmini Mongia. New Delhi: OUP, 2004, Print.

Corry, Stephen. "Modern Times: Loot of Tribal Resources Masquerades as Progress" The Times of India. 10 April 2006. Print.

Das, K.B., and L. K. Mahapatra. Folklore of Orrisa, 1979. New Delhi: NBT, 1999. Print.

Das, Ram Narayan. The Sterling Dictionary of Anthropology. New Delhi: Sterling, 1997. Print.

Dasgupta, Sangeeta. "Recasting the Oraons and the "Tribe: Sarat Chandra Roy's Anthology" (132-171). Anthropology in the East. Founders of Indian Sociology and Anthropology. Eds. Patricia Uberoi et al. Ranikhet: Permanent Black, 2007. Print.

Deshpande, Satish, Patricia Uberoi and Nandini Sunder, eds. Introduction. Anthropology in the East: Founders of Indian Sociology and Anthropology. Ranikhet: Permanent Black, 2007. Print.

Dasgupta, Swapan. "Adivasi Politics in Midnapore, c. 1760-1924" (101-135). 1985. Subaltern Studies. Ed. Ranajit Guha. Vol. IV. New Delhi: OUP, 2005. Print.

Damodaran, Vinita. "Indigenous Forests: Rights, Discourses, and Resistance in Chotanagpur,

1860-2002." Ecological Nationalisms: Nature, Livelihoods, and Identities in South Asia. Ed. Gunnel Cederlof and K. Sivaramakrishnan. New Delhi: Permanent Black, 2005. Print.

Devi, Mahasweta. The Book of The Hunter. Trans. Sagaree and Mandira Sengupta. Calcutta: Seagull, 2002. Print.

Devi, Mahasweta, and Usha Ganguly. Rudali: From Fiction to Performance. Trans. Anjum Katyal. Calcutta: Seagull, 1997. Print.

Devi, Mahasweta. Aranyar Adhikar 1977. Trans. Jagat Shankhdhar. Jangal Ke Davedar. New Delhi: Radhakrishan, 2008. Print.

Devy, Ganesh N. A Nomad Called Thief Reflections on Adivasi Silence. 2006. New Delhi Orient longmn, 2007. Print.

Dharwadkar, Vinay. "English in India and Indian Literature in English: The Early History, 1579-1834" (93-119). Comparative Literature Studies Vol. 39, November 2, 2002. Pennyslyvania: Pennyslyvania State UP. Google Book Search. Web. 23 June 2010.

Dhawan, R. K. The Fictional World of Arun Joshi. New Delhi: Classical Publishig Company, 1986. Print.

Doniger, Wendy. The Hindus. An Alternative History New Delhi: Penguin/ Viking, 2009 Print. Doniger, Wendy, and Brian K. Smith, eds. The Laws of Manu. 1991. New Delhi: Penguin, 2000. Print.

Duyker, Edward. Tribal Guerrillas: The Santals of West Bengal and Naxalite Movement. New Delhi: OUP, 1987. Print.

Dwivedi, Bachaspati. The Santals of West Bengal and Naxalite Movement. New Delhi: OUP, 1987. Print.

Ekka, Philip, "Revivalist Movements Among the Tribals of Chotanagpur" (395-402). The Tribal Situation in India 1972. Ed. K Suresh Singh. Shimla: IIAS, 2002 Print.

Elliott, C.M., ed. Civil Society and Democracy. New Delhi: OUP, 2003. Print.

Ferguson, Niall. Empire: How Britain Made the Modern World. 2003. New Delhi: Penguin, 2008. Print.

Fernandes, Walter. "Informal Economy, Dependence and Management Traditions" (48-69). Continuity and Change in Tribal Society, Ed. Mrinal Miri. Shimla IIAS, 1993. Print.

Fisher, Michael, H. The First Indian Author in English (Dean Mahomed 1759-1851) in India, Ireland and England. New Delhi: Oxford UP, 2000. Google Book Search. Web. 23 June 2010.

The Travels of Dean Mahomet: An Eighteenth Century Journey Through India. Berkely: University of California, 1997. Google Book Search. Web. 23 June 2010.

Foucoult, Michel Discipline and Punish. The Birth of the Prison. 1975. Trans. Alan Sheridan. New York: Vintage Books, 1995. Google Book Search. Web. 12 May 2009.

Foucanit, Michel. The Archaeology of knowledge and the discourse on Language. 1969. Trans. A.M. Sheridan Smith. New York: Pantheon Books, 1982. Print

Frantz, Fanon. The Wretched of the Earth: A Negro Psychoanalyst's Study of the Problems of Racism and Colonialism in the World Today, 1961. Trans. Constance Farrington New York: Penguin, 2001. Google Book Search. Web. 12 May 2009.

Fraser, J.B. Journal of a Tour Through Part of the Snowy Range of The Himalayan Mountains and The Sources of the Rivers Jumna and the Ganges. 1820. New Delhi: Rupa, 2008. Print.

Furer- Haimendorf, C. von. "The Tribal Problem in All-India Perspective." Tribes of India. The Struggle for Survival. New Delhi: OUP, 1982. Print.

Gandhi, Leela. Postcolonial Theory A Critical Indtroduction, 1998, New Delhi OUP, 2005. Print.

Gellner, David N., ed. Ethnic Activism and Civil Society in South Asia: Governance, Conflict and Civil Action. Vol.2. New Delhi: Sage, 2009. Print.

Ghosh, A.K. "Forest Policy In India" (69-84). Ed. Ajay S. Ranat. Indian Forestry A perspective. New Delhi Indus, 1993, Print.

Ghosh, Durba, and D. Kennedy, eds. Decentring Empire: Britain, India and the Transcolonial World. New Delhi: Orient Longman, 2009. Print.

Ghosh, Kaushik "A Market for Aboriginality Primitivism and Race Classification in the Indentured Labour Market of Colonial India" (8-48). Subaltern Studies. 1999. Ed. Gautam Bhadra, Gyan Prakash and Susic Tharu. Vol. X. New Delhi: OUP, 2005. Print.

Gibbon, Edward. The Decline and Fall of the Roman Empire. 1776-1788. Ed. Antony Lentin and Brian Norman. London: Wordsworth, 1998. Print.

Gorky, Maxim. Selected Short Stories. 1959. Crest Publishing House, 2003. Print.

Guha, Ramchandra. "Between Anthropology and Literature: The Ethnography of Verrier Elwin" (330-359).) Anthropology in the East Founders of Indian Sociology and Anthropology. Eds. Patricia Uberoi, Nandini Sunder and Satish Deshpande. Ranikhet: Permanent Black, 2007. Print.

_ _ _. India After Gandhi: The History of the World's Largest Democracy, London: Picador, 2007. Print.

_ _ _. "Forestry in British and Post-British India: A Historical Analysis". Economic and Political Weekly. Vol. 18. No. 44. 1983. Print.

_ _ _. Interview. New Delhi: The Times of India. 11 May, 2007. Print.

_ _ _. Lost in the Woods. Hindustan Times. 15 August 2011. Print.

_ _ _. Savaging the Civilized: Verrier Elwin, His Tribals, and India. Chicago: Chicago UP, 1999. Print.

_ _ _. ed. Social Ecology. New Delhi: OUP, 1998. Print.

_ _ _. The Unquiet Woods: Ecological Change and Peasant Resistance in The Himalaya. 1989. New Delhi: OUP, 1999. Print.

_ _ _."United By Prejudice: How Indians and Americans Look At Each Other Differently". New Delhi: The Times of India. 23 March 2006. Print.

Guha, Ranajit, ed. Subaltern Studies Writings on South Asian History and Society. Vols. I-VI 1982-2005. New Delhi: OUP. Print.

_ _ _. "The Small Voice of History." 1996. Subaltern Studies. Ed.Shahid Amin and Dipesh Chakrabarty. Vol. IX. New Delhi: OUP, 2005. Print.

_ _ _."Dominance Without Hegemony and Its Historiography." Subaltern Studies. 1989. Ed. New Delhi: OUP, 2005. Print.

_ _ _. "The Prose of Counter-Insurgency" (1-42). Subaltern Studies. 1983. Ed. Ranajit Guha. Vol. II. New Delhi: OUP, 2005. Print.

_ _ _. "Discipline and Mobilize" (68-120). Subaltern Studies, 1992. Ed. Partha Chatterjee and Gyanendra Pandey. Vol. VII. New Delhi: OUP, 2005. Print.

Gupta, Dipankar, ed. Sociual Stratification: Oxford in India Reading in Socilogy And Social Anthropology. 2nd ed. New Delhi: OUP, 1992. Print.

Gupta, Ramanika. Yudharata Aam Aadmi: All India Tribal Issue New Delhi: Ramanika Foundation, 2005. Print.

Hardiman, David. "Adivası Assertion in South Gujarat: The Devi Movement of 1922- 3" (57-94). Histories of the Subordinated. New Delhi: Permanent Black, 2006. Print.

Huntington, Samuel. *The Clash of Civilizations*. 1996. New Delhi, Penguin, 1997. Print.

Jadhav, Narendra. Interview. "Caste System Has Become Subtle and Sophisticated" New Delhi: The Times of India, 25 April 2006. Print.

Jain, P.C. Planned Development Amongh Tribals. New Delhi: Rawat Publication, 1999. Print.

Juneja, O.P. Postcolonial Novel: Narratives of Colonial Consciousness. New Delhi: Creative Books, 1995. Print.

Katyal, Anjum, ed. "The Metamorphosis of "Rudali'" (Introductory essay 1-53). Rudali: From Fiction to Performance. By Mahasweta Devi and Usha Ganguly. Calcutta: Seagull, 1997. Print.

Kaviraj, Sudipta, and Sunil Khilnanı, eds. Civil Society: History and Possibilities New Delhi: Cambnidge University Press, 2001. Print.

Keay, John. India: A History. New Delhi: Grove Press, 2001. Print.

Khair, Tabish. In The Shadow of the Empire. India Today, 11 June 2012. Print.

Khilnani, Sunil. The Idea of India. 1997. New Delhi: Penguin, 2004. Print.

Kipling, Rudyard. Stories of India. Ed. Sudhakar Marathe. New Delhi: Penguin, 2003. Print.

Kock, Leon. "Interview With Gayatri Charavorty Spivak: New Nation Writer's Conference in South Africa." A Review of International English Literature. 23(3) 1992 pp.29-47. Google Book Search. Web. 11 May, 2011.

Linkenback, Antje. Forest Futures: Global Representations and Ground Realities in the Himalayas, Ranikhet: Permanent Black, 2007. Print.

Ludden, David. Agricultural Production and South Asian History. 1994. 2 nd. New Delh: OUP, 2005, Print.

Lorimer, Doug. Fundamentals of Historical Materialism: The Marxist View of History and Politics. New Delhi: Aakar, 2006. Print.

Malhotra, Anshu, Gender, Caste and Religioous Identies. 2002. New Delhi: OUP, 2004. Print.

Malinowski, Bronislaw. Sex and repression in Savage Society. 1927. London: Routledge, 2001. Print.

Mansinha, Mayadhar. Fakir Mohan Senapati: Makers of Indian Literature. 1976. New Delhi: Sahitya Akademi, 1997. Print.

Mankad, Piyush. "Seeing Like a State Why Well-Meaning Development Projects Flounder When They Don't Involve End Users in the Process". Indian Express. 08 December 2009. Print.

McLeod, John. Beginning Postocolonialism. Manchester: Manchester University Press, 2000. Print.

Mehta, Gita. A River Sutra. New Delhi: Viking, 1993. Print.

Mitchell, W. "Representation." Critical Terms for Literary Study. Eds. F Lentricchia and T Mc Laughlin. 2nd ed. Chicago: University of Chicago Press, 1995. Print.

Mukherjee, Meenakshi. The Perishable Empire: Essays On Indian Writing in English New Delhi: OUP, 2000. Print.

Muller, F. Max. India: What Can it Teach Us? New Delhi: Rupa, 2002. Print. Marshall, P. J. The Eighteenth Century in Indian History: Evolution or Revolution? New Delhi: OUP, 2003. Print.

Menon, Nivedita. Recovering Subversion: Feminist Polities Beyond the Law. New Delhi Permanent Black, 2004. Print.

Midgley, Mary. Beast and Man: The Roots of Human Nature. 1979. London Routledge, 2002. Print.

Miri, Mrinal, ed. Continuity and Change in Tribal Society. Shimla: IIAS, 1993. Print.

Mishra, K.C. Tribes in the Mahabharata: A Socio-Cultural Study, New Delhi: National, 1987. Print.

Mittal, A.C., and S. P. Sharma, eds. Tribal Women in India Vols. 1-3. New Delhi: Radha Publications, 1998. Print.

Mittal, Kanak. Tribal Identity in Changing Industrial Environment New Delhi: Metropolitan, 1986. Print.

Mohanty, Gopinath. The Bed of Arrows and Other Stories. Trans. Sitakant Mahapatra. New Delhi: Sahitya Akademi, 1995. Print.

Mukherjee, Meenakshi and Harish Trivedi, eds. Interrogating Post colonialism Theory, Text and Context. 1996. Shimla: IIAS, 2000. Print.

Mukherhjee, Mridula. Colonizing Agriculture: The Myth of Punjab Exceptionalism New Delhi: Sage, 2005. Print.

Muller, F.Max. India: What Can It Teach Us? New Delhi: Rupa, 2002. Print.

Mumford, Lewis. The City in History: Its Origins, Its Transformations, and its prospects. New York: Harcourt Brace and World, Inc., 1961. Print.

Nanda, Chandi Prasad. Vocalizing Silence Political Protests in Orissa, 1930-42. New Delhi: Sage, 2008. Print.

Naswa, Sumedha. Tribes of Uttar Pradesh and Uttranchal: Ethnographyt and Bibliographyt of Scheduled Tribes. New Delhi: Mittal Publications, 2001. Print

Nathan, Dev, ed. From Tribe to Caste. Shimla IIAS, 1997. Print.

Narasimhaiah, C.D. English Studies in India: Widening Horizons. New Delhi: Pencraft International, 2002. Print.

Nautiyal, Vidyasagar. Searching for Identity Across the Border. Amar Ujala. Dehradun: 08 October, 2007. Print.

Nayak, Pulin B. "In the Shadow of Growth." New Delhi: The Times of India. 07 April, 2006. Print.

Nehru, Jawaharlal. "Tryst With Destiny" Speech On the Granting of Indian Independence, August 14, 1947. Penguin Book of Twentieth Century Speeches. Ed Brian MacArthur. London: Penguin/ Viking, 1992. Pp. 234- 237. Print.

New York Times. Wild tribes of India Becoming Civilized Lord Curzon's Trip Through Remote Districts. December 22, 1901. Google Book Search Web. 30 June 2008.

Niebuhr, Renhold. Moral Man and Immoral Society A Study in Ethics and Politics 1932. London. Continuum, 2005. Print.

Nongbri, Tiplut. Development, Ethnicity and Gender, New Delhi: Rawat Publications, 2003. Print.

Pati, Biswamoy Situating Social History Orissa, 1800-1997. New Delhi: Orient Longman, 2001. Print.

Patil, Mallikarjun. "Arun Joshi's Fictional Forte." The Novels of Arun Joshi, A Critical Study. Ed. M.K. Bhatnagar. New Delhi: Atlantic Publishers, 2001. Print.

Pollard, D.E.B. Literature and Representation: A Note. British Journal of Aestheties, Vol. 32, No.2. April 1992. Google Book Search, Web. 23 July, 2008.

Pouchepadass, Jacques. 'Subaltern Studies' As Post-Colonial Critique of Modernity." Remapping Knowledge. The Making of Sough Asian Studies in India, Europe und America (19-20th Century). Ed. Jackie Assayag and Veronique Benei. New Delhi: Three Essays Collective, 2004.

Radhakrishna, Meena. Dishonoured by History: Criminal Tribes and British Colonial Policy. New Delhi: Orient Longman, 2001. Print.

Radhakrishnan, S. Indian Philosophy. 1922. Oxford University Press, 1998. 2 vols. Print.

Rajagopal, P.V. Interview. "Settle the Claims of the Tribals to Protect Forests". The Times of India. New Delhi: 11 June 2007. Print.

Ram, Kalpana. "Anthropology as 'Ananthropology': L.K. Ananthakrishna Iyer (1861-1937), Colonial Anthropology, and the 'Native Anthropologist' as Pioneer" (64-105). Anthropology in the East. Founders of Indian Sociology and Anthropology Eds. Patricia Uberoi et al. Ranikhet: Permanent Black. 2007. Print.

Rajagopalachari, C. Mahabharata. 1951. New Delhi: Bhartiya Vidya Bhavan, 2009. Print.

Ratnagar, Shereen. The Other Indians: Essays on Pastoralist Tribal People. New Delhi: Three Essays Collective, 2004. Print. Ray, Niharranjan. Introduction. The Tribal Situation in India. 1972. Ed. K. Suresh Singh. Shimla: IIAS, 2002. Print.

Reddy, Vijay Raghav. Book Review. Doosra Narak Kund by Jaiwanti Dimri. Chhatisgarh Today. October-December 2004. Print.

Roy, Arundhati. The Shape of the Beast: Conversation with Arundhati Roy. Penguin /Viking, 2008). R.Rangachari et el, Large Dams: India's Experience, 2000, a World Commission on Dams (WCD) case study prepared as an input to the World Commission on Dams, Cape town, online at http:// www.dams.org/ Docs/kbase/studies/csinmain.pdf.

Roy, Arundhati. The Shape of the Beast: Conversation with Arundhati Roy. New Delhi: Penguin, 2008. Print.

Roy Burman, B. K. Tribal Situation and Approach to Tribal problems in India. New Delhi: Rajiv Gandhi Foundation. Print.

Roycroft, Daniel J. "Capturing Birsa Munda: The Virtiality of a Colonial era Photograph." Indian Folklore Research Journal, Vol. 1, No. 4, 2004: 53- 68. Print.

Roy, Nilanjana S. "In Midnight's Shadow". Business Standard. 15 July 2008. Print.

Saberwal, V., and M Rajarajan, eds. Battles Over Nature: Science and Politics of Conservation, 2003. New Delhi: Permanent Black, 2009. Print.

Sagreiya, K.P. Forests and Forestry. 1967. New Delhi: National Book Trust, 1994. Print.

Sawant, Shivaji. Mrityunjay. 1974. Trans. Om Shivaraj. New Delhi: Jnanpith, 2000. Print.

Saldanha, Indra Munshi. "Customary Rights and Colonial Regulations. Thana Forests in the Nineteenth Century" (70-84). Continuity and Change in Tribal Society. Ed. Mrinal Miri. Shimla IIAS, 1993. Print.

Sarkar, T. "Jitu Santal's Movement in Malda, 1924-1932: A Study in Tribal Protest" (136-164). Subaltern Studies. 1985. Ed. Ranajit Guha. Vol. IV. New Delhi: OUP, 2005. Print.

Sarkar, M.C. "Customary Rights in Land and Forest of the Tribals in Chotanagpur- Santhal Pargana Region of Bihar" (97-108). Continuity and Change in Tribal Society. Ed. Mrinal Miri. Shimla IIAS, 1993. Print.

Sargreiya, K.P. Forests and Forestry. 1967. New Delhi. National Book Trust, 1964. Print.

Sah, D.C., and Yatindra Singh, eds. Tribal Issues in India. Jaipur: Rawat Publications, 2004. Print.

Sahay, Sarita. Tribal Women in the New Profile Vis-à-vis Their Non-Tribal Twins. New Delhi: Anmol Publication, 2002 Print.

Said, Edward W. Culture and Imperialism. 1993. New York: Vintage, 1994. Print.

_ _ _. *Orientalism*: Western Conceptions of the Orient. 1978 New Delhi: Penguin, 2001. Print.

_ _ _. *Reflections* on Exile and Other Literacy and Cultural Essays. New Delhi: Penguin, 2001. Print.

Salmon, Philip. "Where It Lives." Poetry Society Quarterly. London, 2001. Print.

Senft, Theresa M. *Writing (and) Independence Gayatri Spivak and the Dark Comment of Feminine*, originally appeared in women and performance, Vol. 7. No.2, Issue 14-15, Spring 1995, pp 275-286. Google Book Search. Web. 12 May 2009.

Shaughnessy, M. and J.Stadler. Media and Society: An Introduction. 3rd ed. South Melbourne: Oxford University Press, 2006. Print.

Sills, David L. ed. International Encyclopedia of the Social Sciences, New York: Macmillan/ Free Press, 1968. Vol. 16 (p. 146-151). Print.

Soloinon, Robert C. "Subjectivity", Oxford Companion to Philosophy, OUP, 2005. Google Book Search. Web. 30 August 2008. Sharma, Suresh. Tribal Identity and the Modern World. New Delhi: Sage, 1994. Print.

Shashi, S.S. The Tribal Women of India. New Delhi: Classical Publishing Company, 1991. Print

Simhadri, Y.C. Denotified Tribes. New Delhi: Classical Publishing Company, 1991. Print.

Singh, Katar Rural Development. Principles, Policies and management. 2 nd. ed. New Delhi: Sage, 1999. Print.

Singh, Khushwant. "Opium Eaters." Hindustan Times. 08 June, 2008. Print.

Singh, K.S. "Agrarian Issues in Chotanagpur" (347-359). The Tribal Situation in India. 1972. Ed. K Suresh Singh. Shimla: IIAS, 2002, Print.

Singh K.S. Birsa Munda and His Movement 1874-1901: A Study of a Millenarian Movement in Chotanagpur. 1966. Calcutta: OUP, 1983. Print.

Singh K.S., ed. Our Tribal Heritage: The National Tribal Festival Ranchi: Regional Development Commissioner (Ranchi) and the Anthropological Survey of India, 1989. Print.

Singh K. Suresh, ed. The Tribal Situation in India. Shimla: Indian Institute of Advanced Study, 2007. Print.

Singh, K.S., ed. Tribal Movements in India. Vol 1-2. 1982. New Delhi: Manohar, 2006. Print.

Singh, Pankaj K., ed. The Politics Of Literary Theory and Representation: Writing on Activism and Aesthetics. New Delhi: Manohar, 2003. Print.

Skaria, Ajay. "Writing, Orality and Power in the Dangs, Western India, 1800s 1920s" (13-58). Subaltern Studies. 1996. Ed. Shahid Amin and Dipesh Chakrabarty. Vol. IX. New Delhi: OUP, 2005. Print.

Som, Sujit, and T.B.Suba, eds. Between Ethnography and Fiction: Verier Elwin and the Tribal Question in India. New Delhi: Orient longman, 2005. Print.

Spivak, Gayatri Chakravorty. "A Literary Representation of the Subaltern: Mahasweta Devi's 'Stanadayini'" (91-134). Subaltern Studies, 1987. Ed. Ranajit Guha. Vol. V. New Delhi: OUP, 2005. Print.

_ _ _. "A Literary Representation of the Subaltern: Mahashweta Devi's "Standayini'." Indian Literary Criticism: Theory and Interpretation. Ed. G. N. Devy. New Delhi: Orient Longman, 2002. Print.

_ _ _. "Subaltern Studies: Deconstructing Historiography" (330-363). Subaltern Studies. 1985. Ed. Ranajit Guha. Vol. IV. New Delhi: OUP, 2005. Print.

_ _ _. Trans. Foreword. Choti Munda and His Arrow, 1980. By Mahasweta Devi. Calcutta: Seagull, 2002. Print.

_ _ _. "Discussion: An Afterword on the New Subaltern" (305-335). 2000. Subaltern Studies: Community, Gender and Violence. Eds. Partha Chatterjee and Pradeep Jeganathan. Vol. XI. New Delhi: Permanent Black, 2009. Print.

Srinivas, A. Interview. "Naxalites Today". The Times of India. 11 June 2007. Print.

Srinivas, M.N. Caste: Its Twentieth Century Avatar. New Delhi: Penguin, 1996. Print.

Sudarshan, Anant. So, Are You for the Tigers or the Tribals? The Indian Express. 09 April 2008. Print.

Taradutt. Trihal Development in India: Special References to Orissa. New Delhi: Gyan, 2001. Print.

Thakur, Devendra and Thakur, D.N., eds. Tribal Life in India. Vols. 1-10. New Delhi: Deep and Deep Publications, 1994. Print.

Tribal Women. New Delhi: Deep and Deep, 1995. Thapar, Romila Early India: From the Origins to AD 1300. New Delhi: Penguin, 2002. Print.

Tharoor, Shashi. India: From Midnight to Millenium. New Delhi: Penguin, 1997. Print.

The Times of India." Aboriginal Kids Used as Guinea Pigs in Australia?"16 April 2008. Print.

Tripathi, S.N., ed. Tribal Women in India. New Delhi: Mohit Publication, 2002. Print.

Tulasidas, Goswami Shri Ramacharitamanasa: The Holy Lake of the Acts of Lord Rama. Gorakhpur (UP, India) Gita Press, 2004. Print.

Uberoi, Meera. The Mahabharata. 1996. New Delhi: Penguin, 2005. Print.

Uheroi, Patricia, ed. Family, Kinship and Marriage in India. 1993 New Delhi: Oxford university Press, 2002. Print.

Vachaspati, D. The Fictional Art of Arun Joshi: An Existential Perspective. New Delhi: Atlantic Publishers, 2004. Print.

Vidyarthi, L.P., ed. Tribal Development and its Administration. New Delhi: Concept Publishing Company, 1981. Print.

Vir, Dharam. Tribal Women and Changing Spectrum in India. New Delhi: Classical Publication, 1990. Print.

Vishvanathan Shiv. "On Dissent and Democracy". New Delhi: The Times of India. 25 April 2006. Print.

Walia, Shelley Edward Said and the Writing of History. London: Icon Books, 2001. Print.

Wignaraja, Poona. Women, Poverty and resources, New Delhi: Sage, 1990. Print.

Wright, Gillian. Her Last Hurrah: Book Review of Kamala Markandaya's Bombay Tiger. India Today. 25 February 2008. Print.

Yadav, Kumkum. Tribes in Indian Narratives. Shimla: IIAS, 2003. Print.

Young, Robert J. C. Postcolonialism. A very Short Introduction. New York: OUP, 2003. Print.

Connect with Publisher

Instagram: @wkrishind
Twitter: @wkrishind
Facebook: @wkrishind
Tumblr: @wkrishind
Telegram: @wkrishind

Email: contact@wkrishind.in

                    or

wkrishind@icloud.com

Website: wkrishind.in
WhatsApp: 09999568276